Dawn Holley

22 Keys to Joy

for the easily distracted

Unlock your Mental, Emotional and Spiritual Resilience with God

22 Keys to Joy

for the easily distracted

Unlock your Mental, Emotional and Spiritual Resilience with God

ISBN: 979-8-9890838-0-0
eISBN: 979-8-9890838-1-7

For more information about Guardian Angel Press and our publications, visit our website at

www.guardianangelpress.com.

Dedication

To Jo Ann Huntwork, Lee Holley, and Jeff Reed who left us to meet the Creator of Joy while I found the words to write this book.

Acknowledgments

Nancy Loehr, thank you for being mid-wife, for the birthing of this book through the 3-year gestation period.

At the Dwelling Place Church conference, Dr. James Goll issued a compelling call to action. This book was born from the inspiration drawn from the choices of those faithful attendees.Thank you Andrea and Patrick Penn for hosting this event.

The 21-Day Journey to Joy friends, I love you and the devotional encounter days with Holy Spirit we shared.

Ray and Denise Hughes, for activating hope and creative expectancy with God, my heart sings because of you.

Jim and Mary Baker, for more than I can write here.

The USA/Global Watch family for faithfully praying heaven to earth.

Faith Hope Love House of Prayer, Columbus Ohio for living and modeling a Christ loving covenant community.

My Rock Family (Rock Family Worship Center, in Huntsville Alabama) for teaching presence, service, in humility and love.

Connie Tucker & Father Heart Ministries for activating deep faith, to Trust in God for worship, prayer and life.

Nathan Huntwork, Thank you for suggesting 22 for Jo Ann –Much love to you and Aydin.

My grandmother B.B. and my dad who believed in me and told me repeatedly, I could do anything I set my mind to.

My two sons, Max and George–for the deep joy of being your mom.

Endorsements

Everyone needs encouragement from time to time. But Dawn is "nuther level." She teaches and demonstrates joy as a lifestyle, a true "joyologist." I'm a glad recipient.

Ray Hughes, Author, Storyteller, Poet, and Teacher

———

The mere act of reading this work will put you in a joyful state of mind! Dawn's creative writing style, deep insight and effervescent humor permeate each page. If you go a step farther and actually put into practice her directions, you're in for a major thought-detox that can't help but transform your thinking and regenerate your heart. You'll have the tools to break out of negative thought patterns and truly live out the resilient life of joy you were created to experience.

This isn't just a self-help, slap-a-smile-on-your-face, superficial journey. Dawn speaks candidly about finding joy in the midst of tragedy and the messiness of life. Like finding streams in the midst of the wasteland, no matter what you face in life, you too can experience the abundant life Jesus promised. It all starts with your thought life and this book is a roadmap to those streams in the desert.

Ursula Kemp
CEO, Ulla, Ltd.

———

As you will read in this book, Dr. James Goll's invitation led Dawn to write the devotional, which inspired this book. Both have helped me on my own journey toward inner healing, and the discovery that a personal relationship with Jesus Christ is possible and real! Dawn's framework in the "Journey to Joy" 21-day devotional was instrumental in my breaking the cycle of self-destructive thoughts and word curses. As my journey continues, I rejoice, because of their obedience to the call of God! And I often re-visit these materials!

———

"Dawn of Resilience" is the perfect descriptor for my friend Dawn Holley. The trials in her life, the mountains she has climbed and conquered have only strengthened her and stretched her horizons. Dawn's faith in God was born and developed through adversity and her ability to use her own inner healing to reach others who are hurting. It is beautiful and inspiring. She is a friend to the lonely, a confidant to the faithless, and a voice for those who have lost their words.

Brilliance is the word that comes to mind when I think of Dawn because she is a beacon to all who walk with her in the Light of the One who leads her.

Her "21-day Journey to Joy" is not the only...but a truly effective path to take if you are feeling stuck and need a mentor to guide you into the fullness of what God has for you.

Table of Contents

Acknowledgments   7

Endorsements   9

Introduction   17

Puppies & Balloons   19

   1. Breathe   27

   2. Simple Joys   33

   3. Joy for Courage   35

   4. Thought Fields   39

   5. Power of Words   43

   6. Actions – Simple Attractive Victories   51

   7. Thought Filter   57

   8. Think Deeply -Dream   61

   9. Party in Your Head   65

   10. For + Give   71

   11. Savor Savior – Chocolate Meditation   81

   12. Superpower: Pearl Maker   85

   13. Kind Actions   93

   14. Worship in Life   97

   15. Rest   101

   16. Your Story's Author   109

   17. Harvest & Habits   115

   18. Listen & Learn   125

   19. Community for Eternity   135

   20. Rest and Repeat   137

   21. Rooted: Trees Overcome Together   139

   22. Gold Mine   147

The Road is the Joy   151

Epilogue   153

I will choose to *find joy* in the *journey* God has set before me.

22 Keys to Joy *for the easily distracted*

Introduction

Two people who could be distracted, but chose to have focused, passionate lives are my mom, Lee Holley and Jo Ann Huntwork. Both souls influenced my life and the insights into the keys here. Both left this earth joining the Creator of Joy while I found the words to write this book.

Mom - Lee

My mom was an intense, bright and beautiful steel magnolia. She carried a sharp wit, strong spirit and an amazing laugh most of her days. Living just weeks shy of her 93rd year, her life was a true love story with my dad, sharing nearly 64 years of marriage. She could dance the night away until she couldn't. Her personal thought battles made me a seeker of God at a young age, to keep her laughing, to bring joy and to restore peace. In her later years, olive branches of divine reconciliation were extended weaving us together better than before. God's hand was ever present and working in her life and mine. I am grateful for every battle, scar, tear, and laugh shared with her on this earth. God filled my heart to overflow during the final 15+ years of her life. While her high-profile careers were notable, in her last days she shared her greatest achievement: receiving Jesus as Lord of her life.

Jo Ann

My brave, funny, silly, thoughtful, creative and incredibly organized friend. She had an uncanny ability to glorify what others would consider mundane. A subject matter expert on simple joys.

Frailty and strength resided in her simultaneously. She carried juxtapositions of joy and pain, gain and loss. Her victories were stealth. That is to say, very few knew all she had accomplished in her life. Then there was her cancer diagnosis. I saw such holy courage in her. The kind of courage that got on you and made you braver for knowing her.

Her favorite color was blue. Her favorite number was 2.

I count it one of my highest privileges to have known her well. I loved the Jesus I saw in her. I loved the gold he put in her. From the bottom of my heart, I have witnessed this truth: There is joy, even in trials.

Puppies & Balloons

SILENCING THE CYNIC

I believe my dog has access to limitless joy.

When we met him, he was a gray, shaggy, 1-year-old pup—a new dog with kennel cough in the Franklin County animal shelter.

At 12 and 17, my boys were both taller than me and their kind hearts were hurting. We were all hurting from a five-year long divorce. We arrived at the animal shelter to discover the one they had named Paddington.

I had a list of 3 criteria for my rescue. A 10–12-pound, non-shedding female dog (that doesn't mark territory).

He met none of these.

He was a 25-pound male with a long mop of hair, which shed, and when excited, he peed.

A polite little area rug with a sweet face and short legs.

When we took this fuzzy fella outside, he looked up at me. When I looked down at him, I heard these words,

"We've been through a lot, but it's going to be ok."

A lump formed in my throat. I wanted to wail in deep grieving after the five years of painful persevering.

He was the dog.

Another family had reserved him. Prayerful question to the Lord — Isn't he 'the one' for us?

Two days later, the other family hadn't returned to adopt him and Paddington the pound dog was ours.

He shyly entered my new Camry XLE with cream colored leather. Timid with excitement, he introduced me to dog ownership by puking in the backseat before arriving to his new home.

We named him Pepper. Later he would answer to Baby-Dog and Captain Fuzzy Butte. At this writing, that was 11 years ago.

Pepper was and continues to be a great source of comfort and joy. When it's time for his supper, Pepper's dance is pure joy. He often rides with me in my 2001 SLK convertible, not with his face blowing in the wind, but resting his head on the console between the seats watching me. I look down and see him looking back at me. My heart melts.

Fuzzy friends entertain, interact, and comfort.

He provides a sweet reminder.

Joy is accessible every day.

You are designed for joy. Let that sink in. People who have an optimistic **mindset live longer**[1], have stronger immune systems, and to state the obvious, get more enjoyment out of life. Yet, humans have fallen away from the keys which unlock their full joy design.

Our nation and the world is in a mental health crisis.

The purpose of this book is to offer an invitation into simple changes to unlock the fullness of joy you are designed to experience in your life.

It is simple. It is work. It is intimacy with God.

If I could keep my mom laughing, it would keep her from going to 'the dark side'. Comedy moved me down the path to knowing God, then to teach how to detox from negativity to stay in joy and intimacy with God.

The key to overcoming life's tsunamis is God.

I worked at an insurance company in a high profile position while going through the 5 years of delayed court dates, changing attorneys, heartsick decisions, and all the muck. I was asked to share with the Human

---

1 *https://eraoflight.com/2018/10/27/remove-70-of-toxins-in-your-body-with-this-one-simple-exercise/*

Resources team how I was dealing with stress during the divorce. Hmm. How was I doing it? These keys, when I thought about it, were beginning with my thoughts life, then impacting the words I used, and the actions I was taking. I would be remiss if I failed to mention the dear souls who were praying, loving and encouraging me through those years. If you are one and reading this now, I bless you still.

In Bob Sorge's book, *It's not a Tomb it's a Womb,* he shows how the hurricanes of life can birth something great when partnering with God. For the JOY set before Him, Christ endured the cross. (Emphasis is mine.)

God does not apologize for the trials. Those very trials can correct our character, lead to repentance, and open us up to greater joy when we trust God and His word. He is good.

To unpack His precious gold, we are going to look at a practical joy practice. I am sharing with you, dear reader, 22 keys to unlock your original design to abundant joy.

The Hebrew alphabet is made up of 22 letters which are used to compose the Word of God. The Word of God is called a lamp (Psalms 119:105); thus it is the light by which we are to live.

Joy is strength. God's word has 'joy' or 'rejoice' stated 430 times in the NKJV. Strength and Resilience go hand in hand.

Keys to open up the wealth of God's joy is a treasure hunt. Looking for meanings in numbers is a Hebrew thing. The Hebrew language combines letters and numbers with their symbols. The meaning in these symbols is vast. But we are going to focus on one. The letter "Hey" (ה) This letter represents the power of God's creation, from thoughts, words, and actions.

My friend Jo Ann loved 22. Her birthday was on 22nd. Many of the keys were shared in a 21-day devotional. Jo Ann and I partnered to share 21-Days of Joy to email subscribers during a negativity fast in early 2020. More on that later.

Imagine you're walking in a park on a beautiful day and see a balloon vendor. He is an old man, like the one in the movie *UP*. He gives you a balloon.

Imagine this balloon is some of God's wisdom, the first key of 22. You look down and you are grounded in a beautiful place. This ground is God's truth, your rock and the balloon is yours, as well. Each chapter, you will collect a balloon. As you apply these keys, you will be lifted in spirit and grounded on His Truth as you practice these keys. I believe you will be standing taller in the spirit when you get to the end!

The story in the movie UP is about an old man. He used his balloons to change his grim situation. Those balloons changed his location and took him on the adventure he didn't know he wanted to go on, to become who he had forgotten he was deep inside. Ultimately those balloons awakened him to joy and life. God's wisdom can do the same for us.

Also in UP, we saw distractions. The dogs illustrated these with 'squirrel!' alarms. In my IT days, we used the term 'squirrel' in meetings to acknowledge distractions and get back to the topic.

Haven't seen the movie? You may want to check it out.

Joy is a daily choice. You can choose to walk, to read, to meditate, to journal, to come into intimacy with God. You can choose to be lifted UP, to unlock all the joy God has for you.

Following this 'uplifting' analogy, by the end of this book, you will have 22 balloons to lighten your outlook on life and 22 solid rocks of truth to stand on.

These keys can be applied as frequently as needed. Once you know them, you can use them anytime.

I invite you to take a breath right now and say to yourself: I choose joy.

⸺ ⸻ ⸺

Have you ever repeated something over and over again?

Welcome to declarations. Intentional life affirming declarations targeted to your thought life can introduce change from toxic thoughts to healthy thoughts. You have authority to choose your thoughts.

Declare: I got the power to change my thoughts!

Remember that 90's dance craze song 'I got the power…Everybody dance now'? I danced A LOT to that song. YouTube has a Live version at the Apollo. The length of the video is 4:14. Cross referencing with God's word, a quick Google search produced this verse.

'but whoever drinks the water I give them will never thirst. Indeed, the water I give them will become in them a spring of water welling up to eternal life.'

John 4:14 NIV

We are designed to be wellsprings of JOY.

Make time for God

As you read, plan on using a timer, a bible, a journal, and setting a time each day to be with God. Morning is best for many. After you first read through the book, keep revisiting His keys to deepen and enhance your joy practice.

Holy Spirit can provide direction as to which keys will be part of your daily routine. Some will bless you every day. Some keys you may practice intermittently.

⚜ — ⚜

Ready to commit to take time daily with God? Ask Holy Spirit to help clear five, ten or 30 minutes to invest in your daily practice to build a relationship with your Creator. He wants to meet you and to bring you more joy, peace, faith, patience, hope, self-control and love.

⚜ — ⚜

When establishing a new habit, make it a short time commitment. Use a timer. Expect to enjoy your time. Over time add 1-3 joy keys each morning as time and enjoyment allows. My joy practice is a mix to keep it fun and interesting. This helps a creative mind who is reticent of too much routine. If you enjoy routine, these keys will work nicely as a daily practice. Design your routine.

As we take a look at the first key, you will also learn how these keys were gathered for this book.

1. Breathe

It's easy to take breathing for granted. Breathing happens even if we don't think about it. But we can also intentionally change the way we breathe to relax or increase energy.

In 2020 breathing became a focus. The world was awakened to its importance in that pivotal time.

At the end of a conference in Huntsville Alabama in February 2020, Dr. James Goll invited those attending to do a 21-day negativity/toxic thought fast. (This is right before everything went wonky).

I volunteered to write and share a 21-day devotional to support this negativity fast. Those who signed up to join us received a daily email with a short video linked inside. (The videos are still available as of this writing on @DawnofResilience on YouTube.)

We received many notes of appreciation and requests to do it again during the first 21-Days. We ended up doing the 21-Day "Journey to Joy" a total of three times. I remember three subscribers confessed they were battling suicidal thoughts before we began, and those thoughts lifted during the 21-Days.

This is the power of intimacy with God!

We began before the world shut down, because we set our sights on God, I believe we were able to form a kind of "faith, hope, love bubble" during the pandemic.

In one of the devotionals, I shared:

1.   We are in an atmosphere of fear and isolation.

2.   God loves you and plans to prosper you.

Which one of these do you choose to hang your thought life on?

———

Welcome to the battlefield of the mind. This book shares some testimonies of those saints, their revelations, along with new and enhanced content from the devotionals impacted by my personal journey through some hard things.

———

While helping edit and distribute the email devotionals, precious Jo Ann, got a report her cancer count increased significantly. Bravely and beautifully battling the disease, and effects from experimental drugs and chemo for seven years, my dear friend left us for heaven on August 1, 2021.

My oldest son's battle with depression escalated after Jo Ann's death. He attempted to take his own precious life a few months after her funeral.

My inner circle was shaken, my faith tested. Mom's health declined over the next two years. My dad loved and cared for her, and my oldest son and I helped as needed. Hospice staff blessed us at the end. Her homecoming was in the final minutes of June 13, 2023. In the middle of these sad things, my relationship with God was key to find His peace and strength.

God's mental hygiene is a divine work as we partner with Him in faith. I believe He does a kind of 'mental floss'. Dental care is important, too, but I digress.

Declare: "I am receiving all His benefits and Holy Spirit-wise counsel. I will look to God for help and receive His radiant Joy for strength." see

Ps. 34:5

What about BREATHING, Dawn? Ah yes.

There is power in deep healing breath. I had practiced this for decades. I developed a Healing Movement class in 2015 aligning movement with diaphragmatic breathing. I continue teaching this class today via Zoom. As I researched breathing for the devotional, I was surprised to learn how much power to detoxing our bodies is in our lungs.

The gift of breath is something we can somewhat control or do without thinking. The choice to do deep breathing enables our lungs to **purge 70% of toxins**[1] from our body. Breath is truly life.

Meditation: (If you're able, speak these words out loud as you take your breaths.) Today I'm intentionally breathing. By design, I inhale with my 'great-full lungs' to live. I exhale tension, stress, and toxins to live. Thankful to take in another breath, I am alive. God breathed life into Adam. God is with me now.

YHWH is a Hebrew word for God. The two syllables have been referenced as the **breath of life**[2]. Gen. 2. 'Yah' inhale. 'Weh' the exhale. Ancient Jewish wisdom presents that our Creator is being declared with each breath.

---

1. *https://eraoflight.com/2018/10/27/remove-70-of-toxins-in-your-body-with-this-one-simple-exercise/*
2. *https://yrm.org/breathing-the-name-yahweh/*

"Let everything that has breath praise the Lord."
Ps. 150:6 NIV

When I breathe into my belly, I am breathing in healing—literally. Belly breath (diaphragmatic breathing) stimulates the immune system and calms the fight or flight response (to reduce or eliminate unhealthy stress). Our thoughts on life are improved, too. Today I breathe. We often don't appreciate our health until we are sick. I am more alive today because I am celebrating the simple joy of breath.

Declaration - I open my heart and mind to this simple joy of life. I breathe in more smiles and exhale worries. I have my breath. Today I choose to fill my lungs and my day with simple joys. Even when things are hard, I can breathe, I can smile, and I can laugh. I will forgive myself if I forget this truth. I can always start again to find more simple joys. I will continue to breathe healing breath, knowing there are many simple joys each day.

Joy Key: Breath is life.

2. Simple Joys

Breathing is a simple joy. Smiling, laughter of a loved one, tuning to beauty in nature, are all simple joys pointing to YHWH. As your mind is renewing through simple joys, be intentional about your healing breath. Detox in breathing helps your mind, too!

There is great power in Words. I remember *The Help*, a movie where a little girl was told, *"You are smart. You are kind. You are important."* We can use this simple tool to boost our life force. After all, the power of life is in the tongue. If we write and say life-affirming words, we are reminded of our true identity. This triggers the brain to adjust to match thoughts to the words. Unfortunately, the contrary is also true. For example, if you catch yourself thinking and saying, "I always lose my keys" Stop. Rethink and rephrase to a better outcome. "I find my keys and always put them in this place." (Challenge yourself to connect your thoughts and words to a better habit and a better future.)

"I am…" statements are declarations. Declarations are key to taking back the joy you're designed to carry. Shedding toxic thoughts is a matter of replenishing your thought life with healthy thoughts. As you keep your thoughts set on how God sees you, your passion and purpose will rise up. When this happens it actually helps your immune system. "I am…" statements strengthen the true you. So much around us are distractions from God's love and the journey of who you are becoming. To be clear, you are now AND you are becoming a fuller, more courageous and joyful you, as you grab your heavenly keys.

Think of three simple and powerful words—two life affirming words you identify with now and one you're working on to identify with in your future.

What two simple and powerful words do you identify with today? What word would you like to be identified with in the future? As your brain agrees with the first two simple powerful words, it begins to recalibrate to send ideas to align with the third simple powerful word. You are speaking the truth. Repeat as needed.

Some simple powerful word ideas: Healthy. Calm. Creative. Clean. Courageous. Fun. Joyful. Honest. Helpful. Strong. Wise. Funny. Thorough. Innovative. Peaceful. Artistic.

Five-minute ACTION:

Take five minutes and write and say your three "I am…" statements. Try it in front of a mirror. Keep saying, declaring the truth for now and your future.

Joy Key: See God's beauty in the simple truth

3. Joy for Courage

"I am leaving you with a gift—peace of mind and heart. And the peace I give is a gift the world cannot give. So don't be troubled or afraid."
John 14:27 NLT

We are peace carriers, conquering fear.

I want to take you back to a mind battle in 1993. After 36 hours of painful contractions, I was questioning my wisdom in choosing natural childbirth. I don't remember the pain now, but I do remember the moment when fear entered the scene. It was when the thought, 'women die in childbirth', came into my head. All of me was ready to give up, my thoughts were anxious, exhausted and distracted from the task to birth a child. Too weak to do much, my groans sought God. He met me there. There was a shift. They offered me a local spinal 'block'. Yes! Please!

About fifteen minutes after they administered the anesthesia, my mental state went from 'I may die trying to give birth' to singing show tunes. Specifically, like Ethyl Merman, singing 'There's no business-like show business'

Max was born on the 21 of November at 3:38 a.m. officially making me a mom.

'the son of Enosh, the son of Seth, the son of Adam, the son of God.'
Luke 3:38

"...give thanks in all circumstances; for this is God's will for you in Christ Jesus."
Thessalonians 5:18 NIV

One scripture aligned with Max's time of birth, the other is just true.

"For the joy set before him, he endured the cross..."
Hebrews 12:2b NIV

For the joy set before this mom to bring life into the world, I endured the pain and thank God for the intrathecal morphine 'spinal block' that day.

Heads up. There is a demonic agenda wanting to torment your thoughts and take you out: killjoy. This can show up in a toxic thought, which can become worry and anxiety. Thoughts that are not from God, may already be inside your head, and are trying to get in your head. These thoughts are trying to steal your joy, your identity, your purpose, and exhaust you to surrender to a lifeless walk. Demonic agenda: get every human being sin-focused and oppressed, depressed and powerless. This is NOT you or God's plan for you. If you are thinking that way, stop it…right now.

OK– that's my Mama Bear coming out.

But it's true. God has a better view, a better plan, a better life than that yucky toxic thought soup of fear, doubt, and anxiety!! You are called for purpose and to walk in God's power and truth. You won't see life as a gift if you're in a muddy soup of self-doubt, bitterness, resentment, fear, anxiety, despair, and sadness.

There is a time for grieving. I know this all too well this season. But grieving is for a time, it isn't a place to stop and build a residential development. It is a place for a season to visit, then gracefully exit.

As a child of God, you are in the victory of the One who went before you. The author of love and eternal truth will help you through the valley seasons. I pray we fellow saints will rise up and help each other in these seasons, to be reflections of His loving ways.

His Word, supporting friends, and simple joys can shift your perspective to one of gratitude.

Five-minute ACTION:

Take five minutes and challenge yourself to make a gratitude list. If your gratitude list is sarcastic, try it again and get to sincere reasons you can thank God for your life. Gratitude can be stated as you're driving, or walking. Whenever you can, say them out loud. Open your prayers with gratitude.

Joy Key: When things are grim, choose to seek Him; let gratitude in.

4. Thought Fields

Our thought life is vast. We have so many thoughts in a day, thoughts/synaptic transactions, **number in the thousands to tens of thousands**[1], depending on how you measure them.

Prayer: Lord, thank you for thinking of us, mere mortals, human beings you care for, you made us only a little lower than You and crowned us with glory and honor. (Ps. 8)

May my thoughts of YOU overwhelm me where I am today. Meet me with Your unfailing love, eternal hope, and steadfast strength to renew my thoughts. I pray a revelation of the magnitude of Your greatness to shine brighter than any dark thought. Lord, your thoughts for me are good, and far larger than any heavy thing I carry, so I release my toxic thought burdens to you.

Lord, thank you for taking these burdens so I can evict the toxic thoughts, and instead meditate on Your love, hope, and strength. *Amen.*

The 2020 Negativity fast/Toxic Thought Detox brought in testimonies from new and old friends.

> I am enjoying the 21-Day Detox Journey. I have found my Day
> 1 words are having a greater impact than I had anticipated. My
> negative self-judgment is decreasing. Thank you for taking us on
> this journey. E., Alabama

When your true design is awakened, you realize YOU are a precious part of THE SOLUTION by just being you + God. The awakened you is powerful. The TRUE YOU is part of Holy Spirit enlightened strategies to shift atmospheres, to bring hope to what this day and this season holds.

Open your heart. Speak LIFE over yourself. Say three "I am…" statements today. As you grow comfortable with God's truth about you, you will grow healthy thoughts. Journal your declarations, gratitude thoughts, and simple joys. Say them daily until your thoughts and words are in harmony with God's truth. Try saying or thinking your three I am words with something you do throughout the day, like going to the bathroom, drinking a beverage, petting your dog, etc.

He wants you to choose His thoughts and words daily!

My husband's three words are: Healthy, Helpful and Prayerful, and mine are Courageous, Competent and Confident. For him, prayer was for the purpose of becoming a greater Prayer Warrior. For mine, Confident because I want to be more confident when I speak or share something from the Word. Also, I don't want to let the enemy intimidate me that I have missed it, or that others around me whom 'I perceive' as more spiritually mature will judge me 'incompetent' in the Word. (Of course, I want my own pride to be mitigated by my heart's desire to rightly divine the Word.) Philippians 4:8 is the goal!

Thank you for leading us on this significant journey! The timing is especially God-ordained. It would be so good to have everyone doing this. M., Colorado Springs, CO

Joy Key: Take authority to re-focus thoughts to tune them to God's greater thoughts.

22 Keys to Joy *for the easily distracted*

5. Power of Words

Words are powerful. Words influence the life you will lead, the people you will know, the quality of love you will experience. Word seeds influence what your life will harvest. They illustrate what you have been meditating on and what is in your heart. Words can also recalibrate thoughts to overcome a limited, boxed in mindset.

Declare: I receive all God has for me today. I believe He is with me, healing me and helping me to love Him as He loves me, so I can be the child of God He designed me to be.

Declarations: (list your three life affirming identity words. These can change, be added to, but be consistent until you have reached the belief to claim the "new you" word, the third word listed.)

I am…

I am…

I am…

I am leaving you with a gift—peace of mind and heart. And the peace I give is a gift the world cannot give. So don't be troubled or afraid.
John 14:27 NLT

One thing I recommended during the negativity fast/Toxic Thought Detox was to take communion daily. This formed a habit many of us continue to this day.

It is amazing to read God's word out loud. I was first introduced to this on the National Day of Prayer in downtown Huntsville. In the early morning hours, I joined brothers and sisters in faith around the courthouse. Receiving a slip of paper with a section of the Bible to read, I took my place in the circle, social distanced, and read the Word out loud. Not shouting, just audible. I learned if enough people participate, the entire Word of God can be released in an hour or two.

I discovered a cool thing when I volunteered the first year. I volunteered to read segment after mine. A lengthy time of reading the Word out loud, I experienced the Lord speaking to me and giving me greater revelations of His Word as I read. I read well over an hour that day, but even five minutes out loud is beneficial. I invite you to try this for five minutes over several days. Early morning is a great time. After practicing this for a while, see if you notice a difference in your closeness to God. It has blessed me over and over again. You may follow a reading plan to complete the bible in a year. I often use an app to listen to the Word as I sleep. These days I ask God what He wants me to read. I open to chapter and verse and go from there. Not hearing anything specific? Start in Psalm 139, John or Matthew, and just keep reading.

When I take a processed food and sugar fast, my appetite changes. I break the sugar habit and crave whole foods. As you establish a 'eating His Word' habit, you will hunger for His wisdom. He loves you and wants you to draw closer to Him. Practice this for joy for life.

In 2020, during our 21-Day Thought detox/negativity fast I read specific verses out loud daily.

I declared Psalm 91 and Psalm 103:1-5 protection and blessings over us, over our families, those around us, over our nation, Israel and the world.

Whoever dwells in the shelter of the Most High
will rest in the shadow of the Almighty.
I will say of the Lord, "He is my refuge and my fortress,
my God, in whom I trust."
Surely he will save you
from the fowler's snare
and from the deadly pestilence.
He will cover you with his feathers,
and under his wings you will find refuge;
his faithfulness will be your shield and rampart.
You will not fear the terror of night,
nor the arrow that flies by day,
nor the pestilence that stalks in the darkness,
nor the plague that destroys at midday.
A thousand may fall at your side,
ten thousand at your right hand,
but it will not come near you.
You will only observe with your eyes
and see the punishment of the wicked.
If you say, "The Lord is my refuge,"
and you make the Most High your dwelling,
no harm will overtake you,
no disaster will come near your tent.
For he will command his angels concerning you
to guard you in all your ways;
they will lift you up in their hands,
so that you will not strike your foot against a stone.
You will tread on the lion and the cobra;
you will trample the great lion and the serpent.
"Because he loves me," says the Lord, "I will rescue him;
I will protect him, for he acknowledges my name.

He will call on me, and I will answer him;
I will be with him in trouble,
I will deliver him and honor him.
With long life I will satisfy him
and show him my salvation.

Psalm 91:1-16 NLT

Bless the Lord, O my soul;
And all that is within me, bless His holy name!
Bless the Lord, O my soul,
And forget not all His benefits:
Who forgives all your iniquities,
Who heals all your diseases,
Who redeems your life from destruction,
Who crowns you with lovingkindness and tender mercies,
Who satisfies your mouth with good things,
So that your youth is renewed like the eagle's.

Psalm 103:1-5, NLT

I meditated on Psalm 103 for many years. I prayed this over Jo Ann when she had her cancer diagnosis. I believed in her miraculous healing and we did see miracles. Not all the ones I had believed for, but, Praise God, seven more years on earth, where I was deeply moved by her inspirational walk in faith.

—⁕———⁕—

Five-minute ACTION 1:

Take five minutes and read the Word of God out loud. Hearing His word is a joy key. You can start in John, Psalms 100, Genesis, or where ever you choose. Ask God for new revelations as you read His Word out loud.

Five-minute ACTION 2:

Take time with God. Find a ritual of prayer and communion that works into your daily routine. Give yourself grace as you develop this new habit. Consider the early morning hours. Invite him to join you for a cup of coffee or tea. Make Him a cup, sit in near a chair where you will rest and imagine He is with you. He is. Be with Him. Begin by reading His word. Try listening or journaling as you experience His word. The following is a testimony of the fruit of this practice I shared on social media.

—⁕———⁕—

"Last night, in the hospital room with mom, I was reading the book of Matthew (1-6) to her as she was resting. She had been sedated because she was confused and agitated.

As I read - she became lucid. She told me her grandmother would read the bible to her when she was young. She told me her grandmother was a praying woman, always reading the Word. My mom didn't talk about her faith when we were growing up. I asked what she would consider her most important life achievement? She said her grandmother would

say her belief in Jesus as her savior as the most important thing.

And I asked, Do you agree with your grandmother?

She responded in full mom character, 'Of course, why wouldn't I?'

Grateful for this moment - a true gift."

Joy Key: Read the Word out loud every day.

6. Actions – Simple Attractive Victories

Actions. Every day is filled with them. The human brain simplifies all the actions into rituals, habits, and systems to administer the order and priorities to keep the body living. To our brain, avoiding pain and discomfort is a priority. In brain language, status quo is easier than change. To combat toxic thinking, we need strategies to switch our brain to override the status quo and establish healthier thoughts for a better life.

In *Atomic Habits*, author James Clear offers readers a way to reset our less-than-best habits.

Make the target easy.

Practice a simple habit over and over. Gain small victories over and over. After a small victory, build on it. This has proven more successful for your brain to adopt small steps. It is good to have a big hairy goal, but daily habits are the key to get there. A simple target. Just 1% better every day. Science shows more gain over time with this strategy. To keep going, make the new habit attractive.

Applying this 1% simple habit rule, over the course of a lifetime you will have significantly improved your life skills. In *Atomic Habits,* Clear shares about a friend who used a future identity word, "Healthy" to change her lifestyle.

I am Healthy. She began making her decisions asking herself what would a healthy person do. "Would a healthy person order a burrito or a salad?" "Would a healthy person jump in a cab or walk to that meeting?"

She effectively changed her life trajectory by identifying as a healthy person in many small decisions.

Consider your third word in your three word "I am…" statements. You are moving yourself to align with this future identifier. To apply this, ask yourself *what would a person with that attribute do?* James' friend made a decision to be healthy. This identifying with "healthy" in thought then led to words by asking decision- making questions. Decisions were changing her small daily actions to line up with "healthy." She lost 100 pounds by retraining her thoughts to identify with 'I am healthy'.

You will face The Accuser as you progress. Tempting you away from God's best, tempting you to stop fueling your future good, to distract your focus. Ask God to help you with Holy Spirit led Self-Control.

The evil one will try to stop you, to turn off the powerful transformation happening with the "I am…" statements. Combat this by imagining your success. What do you feel like? What is your life like in this future state? You will have deeper commitment for the joy set before you when you imagine your successful future state. Keep going and tweaking and moving 1% toward your new identity. By celebrating small victories, you are practicing for lifelong joy by agreeing with God as He sees you.

In the going deeper, you may meet triggers from your past. Your past is covered by His blood. Yeshua/Jesus paid his life for your life to be fully free. Love Him and seek Him. As a child of God, don't look at your past, except under the blood. Freedom in Him. Mama Bear here: I invite you take authority of your thoughts to receive and believe in Yeshua/Jesus.

Our 21-day devotional shared insights around three superpowers most folks don't fully activate. These super powers influence the trajectory of your life and will ultimately write your life book.

The Power of Thoughts.

The Power of Words.

The Power of Actions.

A quote attributed to Margaret Thatcher, and many others, carries a simple path to destiny.

> Watch your thoughts, they become your words;
>
> watch your words, they become your actions;
>
> watch your actions, they become your habits;
>
> watch your habits, they become your character;
>
> watch your character, for it becomes your destiny.
>
> *Author unknown*

When I see this road map, I see a plan. I can choose to reset as needed so I can keep going.

> *God says there are new mercies every day. 'The steadfast love of the Lord never ceases; his mercies never come to an end; they are new every morning; great is your faithfulness.'*
> *Lam. 3:22-23 NLT*

God loves us and encourages us to keep learning how to honor Him with our lives. Specifically with thoughts, words, and actions, to honor Him with another best choice day.

Ask yourself, 'Can I do a 1% day today?' Most days, the answer is yes.

You may be thinking 'Dawn, will God stop loving me if I don't improve 1%?'

Well, beloved, God's steadfast love is more solid-state than my KitchenAid mixer. And that mixer never stops working. Kind of like the song 'Way Maker, even when we can't see it, He's working.'

Isn't it freeing to know our God is loving and forgiving mistakes as we seek to love and honor Him?

It is important to embrace this as we set out on this quest for intimacy with God and His abundant joy. Why? Because when we set to do new things, we are guaranteed to:

- do it wrong

- do it small without anyone noticing

- do it rough

- do it afraid

- do it and feel foolish

Action crushes fear and creates clarity.

Jaime Cross

Keep seeking Him and growing. You are unlocking the wells of joy and peace to awaken the actions for your breakthrough.

Joy Key: Celebrate small victories

7. Thought Filter

Our water is filtered to be healthy to drink. Our thoughts can be filtered to be healthy to drink in, too. Today we declare our Thought Filter.

Whatever is true, whatever is noble, whatever is right, whatever is pure, whatever is lovely, whatever is admirable – if anything is excellent or praiseworthy – think about such things.

Philippians 4:8 NIV

This is declared in the room when I speak at corporate events on the subject of Resilience. This scripture is the 'training wheels' to run the race with God in joy. If you seek God's face, trusting Him in every facet of your life, you will see these at work.

Sure, you will see the wickedness of man. But we know by these wise words how to find the God in the situation. We especially need this now.

Here's the devotional on the Thought Filter from our Journey to Joy.

You are not your thoughts. Today gently observe how your thoughts align with the thought filter. Not judging, just observing. Prepare to release what doesn't belong in our divine design.

Five minute ACTION:

Thank you, Lord, for all these blessings:

(Insert your simple joy treasures of gratitude.)

Lord, show me where I'm out of alignment with your thoughts. Help me with my unbelief. Give me Your word of truth over any lie I have let into my thoughts. Holy Spirit help me exchange those lesser thoughts with Your words of truth. Your Word, Lord, trumps the lies of the enemy. Renew my thoughts as I agree with Your greater truth. I rise above the lesser thoughts of heaviness, sadness, shame, fear, depression, anxiety, doubt, anger, bitterness, greed, and deception. I am in the beauty of Your glorious presence. You are great and worthy of my praise.

So I will praise you today, and always, in Jesus' name. Amen.

⁂

Write the Thought Filter on your heart to change thoughts to align with God's truth.

Whatever is true, whatever is noble, whatever is right, whatever is pure, whatever is lovely, whatever is admirable – if anything is excellent or praiseworthy – think about such things.

Philippians. 4:8 NIV

Choose Joy.   There is a stealer of joy. Killjoy.

Keep the truth waters flowing through your thoughts to flush the toxic killjoy thoughts out. Each declaration adds to the tuning of your thoughts. Receive abundant truth. Read Psalm 139. Know God is singing these over you, and more!

Joy Key: Apply the Phil. 4:8 Thought Filter.

22 Keys to Joy *for the easily distracted*

8. Think Deeply -Dream

We are designed to think deeply. Since our culture doesn't allow 'bandwidth' for this deep thinking we can become easily distracted. It's time to take authority over thoughts by focusing on what pleases God.

"Show me your checkbook and your calendar, and I will tell you about your walk with God."

Billy Graham

Intentionally carving out time to think deeply, and align thoughts with His promises, pleases God.

I live in Alabama on a mountain called Monte Sano (Spanish for mountain of health). As I am writing I am looking out on lots of trees. When I began sharing Resilience (how to bounce toxic thoughts out for a thriving thought life), I dove into the research of Dr. Caroline Leaf, a Christian neuroscientist.

As Dr. Leaf explains with two models, thoughts create tree patterns in the brain. The toxic thoughts look like sickly trees. The healthy thought patterns look like healthy trees.

Let's smile that this researcher's name is Leaf.

Joy is fed by meditating on the goodness of God.

When we activate our sanctified imagination to dream with God, we have an opportunity to explore 'With God All things are Possible'.

Fear Not

If you have ever worried about something, you know how to meditate on toxic thoughts.

Here we shift perspective. Ask God to help. What if God gave you every desire He put on your heart? Apply the Thought Filter (Phil. 4:8) and DREAM. Prepare to write out your 'Anything is Possible' dreams in your journal.

Call to Action: Keep this dream exercise to 5-10 minutes. With your journal in hand, settle into your quiet place. Before you begin, consider these words from **Ray Hughes**[1].

God designed music, worship, and creativity to awaken the true you to experience the true Him. Abandon the boundaries you have erected around your personality.

Today is the day that you cease to protect yourself by guarding your dreams and hiding your heart. Today is the day to sing the new song that is the new you. Creativity, music, and true worship happen when

---

1.https://selahonline.teachable.com/

silence tells its dreams.

For art, especially music, is the most confident voice of silence. Tell God your dreams as part of your expressed discipline. Sing your dreams, paint your dreams, dance your dreams, write your dreams, sculpt or carve or make jewelry while you dream out loud. Turn your pottery wheel into a dream machine.

Dream in every key or chord or note that you can play on your instrument. Let the true you break the silence today. Let God hear the true you — out loud — as a vocabulary of worship.

Ray Hughes

Declare your three words and put Phil. 4:8 in that declaration. Set your timer for 10 minutes. When the time begins, write your dreams swiftly. Let the dreams flow onto your journal. No limits, no prioritization. Feed your overcomer spirit by writing your list of life dreams. Float above obstacles, like an eagle soaring with a clear vision of great things to come. Whatever is lovely and honorable, beautiful and praiseworthy, pour these thoughts onto these pages. Be positive and unhindered on your dream page.

What is your relationship with God? Have children, grandchildren, great-grands? What do you want for them? Who is with you? What do you do for fun? For fitness? Let God give you a glimpse of His plans.

Imagine a very positive future. Keep this activity up until the timer stops.

Idea Seeds for your Dream Page	
Hobbies	Achievements
Where you want to live	Things you want to have in your life
Pets	People you want to meet
Where you want to travel	Impact on family/ community/state/nation
What you do for fun	What you do for physical fitness

"I loved today's devotion … It made my heart (and all of me) happy!" L., Grove City, Ohio

Joy Key: Seek His View and Dream.

9. Party in Your Head

I will place on his shoulder the key to the house of David; what he opens no one can shut, and what he shuts no one can open.

Isaiah: 22:22, NIV

We have a HUGE party in our heads. Tens of thousands of thoughts are attending this party. Worry, fear, and anxiety want to come to the party. If we let them in, they'll take over. Then it's not such a great party in our heads anymore. Our head is on our shoulders. God has a plan.

God designed us to have a thought bouncer. We're designed to keep this party in our heads a beautiful party, full of hope, kindness, peace, and joy most of the time. So how do we manage to keep the unwanted toxic guests out of the party in our heads? We add the Fruit to this guest list. Not the Fruit of the Loom guys...but the Fruit of the Spirit.

Pray.

Christian neuroscientist Dr. Caroline Leaf notes:

"It has been found that 12 minutes of daily focused prayer over an 8-week period can change the brain to such an extent that it can be measured on a brain scan."

Remember my 36 hours of labor with my first born? I groaned a prayer, and He answered.

Prayers don't have to be complicated

"Lord, I love you. Please help me today."

He wants to meet you wherever you are on your faith walk. He loves you unconditionally with agape love.

A gratitude practice changes our heart to receive more of God's promises. We humbly invite greater plans than our natural thoughts could conjure up. We fill our thought party with His thoughts about us. We can take His Word and apply it like a bouncer to get the toxic thoughts out of our heads. When we think deeply, we can exchange our toxic-thought 'guests' for the ones we're designed to party with – like joy, peace, faith, hope, patience, perseverance, and self-control. Self-control is one I love to be well acquainted with…it can be the best bouncer at the party. Holy Spirit will answer when I cry out for self-control with a repentant heart. When we lean on Holy Spirit, we can do hard things. He's the Wise One helping us make right choices, to filter thoughts, words, and actions in our lives to align with God.

The executive portion of your brain is the prefrontal cortex. It makes decisions on how to process things. When trained, it can keep the negative emotions from taking over the party. We will experience hard things, but our emotions are not designed to rule.

Worry will knock at the door, but we don't have to let it in.

My youngest son and I began a practice of early morning declarations when he was in middle school. This habit was inspired by our pastor James Baker's declaration practice he did with his sons.

⁂

"To wake me for school, my mom would throw open my door every morning and task me with a series of questions, such as: "What is your name?" "Who are you?" "What is your mission?" The answers to these led me down a path of declarations, saying my name, that I am a son of a king and that my purpose is to bring heaven to earth and see Jesus get his full reward.

When the struggles of life arise, there are always new and creative ways to doubt and fret, but in my calling, my identity and in all of the areas where I declared purpose in those early mornings, I remain steadfast and sure."

George Reed

❧ —·— ❧

Meditation/Declaration: I am loved by my Creator. He is good and wants good things for me. I will apply the Philippians 4:8 "Thought Filter" to my thoughts. Today I choose to be grateful for simple joys. I don't invite toxic thoughts to the party in my head. I bounce them by choosing healthy thoughts. I am inviting God's love and promises to the party in my head today and every day.

❧ —·— ❧

Power of Words –

Let the Redeemed of the Lord, say so…

Ps. 107:2

❧ —·— ❧

Read your dream page(s) and ask God to renew your mind to think more on the dreams. Ask what 1% you can take toward a dream. God dreams with you (Jeremiah 29:11) Jesus is on your prayer team. Holy Spirit is with you. (Romans 8:34, Romans 8:26-27, Hebrews 7:25).

You're designed to win.

Five-minute ACTION x2:

Take 10 minutes to journal. Set your timer for 10 minutes, breathe, declare your three simple powerful words, and pray about one of your dreams, then journal.

God's Mental Hygiene is evicting Stinkin' Thinkin'!

Your ministry is just amazing! I am still so thankful that God has given birth to your ministry in such a time as this. Thank you for the devotionals and videos! - C., Double *Springs, AL*

Joy Key: Grow your prayer life to grow your relationship with God.

10. For + Give

For + Give = Detox from Bitterness

Let's take a look at a heart matter from a heart perspective.

On 3/6/2020, I received this text: "Self-sufficiency is a dangerous illusion which leads to self-destruction. May our country never forget we need our Creator, our God."

in all your ways submit to Him, and He will make your paths straight.
Prov. 3:6

I pray we are also awakened to how much we need each other.

Jesus declared, 'Love the Lord your God with all your heart and with all your soul and with all your mind.' This is... the greatest commandment. And the second is like it: 'Love your neighbor as yourself.'

Matthew 22:38-39 NLT

We are all interconnected. It is even written in nature. Think of the delicate balance of ecosystems. Consider the honey bees. Without them, life is not so sweet. Honey pun aside, bees are an integral part of the ecosphere. It is estimated bees are responsible for pollinating 80% of our food sources. You remove one part of the ecosystem and the whole of life is threatened.

You matter to God and to this interconnection with all mankind and all life on earth.

God loves the world and each one of us in it. God rejoices when one heart opens to receive Him. His love, His forgiveness, if we truly experience it, brings not only transformational love, and sound mind.; it is contagious. Infectious viral love and forgiveness. With Him, we can forgive.

***

"Give, and you will receive. Your gift will return to you in full—pressed down, shaken together to make room for more, running over, and poured into your lap. The amount you give will determine the amount you get back."
Luke 6:38 NLT

The quote on self-sufficiency at the beginning of this chapter is a wakeup call to the United States. In 2020, there was conflict and offense in the streets and in many hearts. Unforgiveness isolates us from God and each other.

Practicing swift forgiveness every day leads the way to intimacy with God. God cannot work His great work in us without forgiveness. With swift forgiveness, we can truly love our neighbors as ourselves.

It is our choice to engage in the cycle of giving and receiving God's generous gift of forgiveness. I pray that you are ready. Abba is taking us on a heart journey today.

For + Give = Detox from Bitterness. If you don't feel you have any unforgiveness, ask God if He can help reveal any offensive feelings you have toward people in your life. Maybe the person who cut you off on the freeway on your way to buy groceries, or the one who cut in line at the grocery store, or yelled at you for cutting in line when you weren't in line. Clearly, a good portion of my time is spent getting groceries.

Thank you, God for provision for all your people.

In 1 Chronicles 28:9, Solomon receives this sage advice: "…serve Him with wholehearted devotion and with a <u>willing mind</u>, for the Lord searches every heart and understands every desire and every thought. If you seek him, he will be found by you…" (emphasis is mine)

Imagine this truth: Being fully loved by God. Simple Joys begin to train our hearts to be grateful. Let's go deeper into our hearts.

Blessed are the pure in heart, for they shall see God.

Matthew 5:8 NLT

Dr. Charles Thurston, an Emergency Medicine Specialist, shares how our anatomy aligns with the Word of God.

His observations include how God's Word is demonstrated in the heart's four chambers.

All mammals and birds have four-chambered hearts. The heart functions to keep blood circulating. Simply put the heart receives, then gives blood back to the rest of the circulatory system. Dr. Thurston describes in greater detail what I simplify here. Each of the four chambers has a role. As Dr. Thurston's revelation unfolds, the first blesses the blood—as it is received into the atrium chamber, the second honors the blood, the third glorifies it (the blood is oxygenated), and the fourth gives it power to leave the heart and circulate in the body. The door-like ventricles beat out life's song.

Blessing. Honor. Glory. Power. Every heartbeat.

All these chambers renewing our life-giving blood. Because of his deep understanding of anatomy and the word, Dr. Chuck Thurston saw connection between the roles of the four chambers of the heart and the vision of heaven St. John wrote in Revelations 5:13, all the creatures proclaim 'blessing, honor, glory and power.'

"Let everything that has breath praise the Lord."
Psalm 150:6.

A heart is giving and receiving blood, with blessing, honor, glory, and power as our heart beats life… We are doing on earth what John observed in heaven.

————

You may be thinking, Dawn…what's this got to do with forgiveness? Great—you're still with me.

Here's something to ponder. Give is in forgiveness. To receive, there is giving.

Hearts are designed to give and receive. Hearts are giving oxygen and nutrients to the blood returning to the heart. As the heart receives blood that has cycled through our body, the heart navigates this blood to the lungs, giving it breath (oxygen), and then gives the blood back to the circulatory system to keep our life going. A heart receives and gives, receives and gives, receives and gives, circulating our blood for us to live.

God cares about our hearts and our thoughts. He makes it very clear: to receive forgiveness, we must forgive. He designed our hearts to give and receive

We receive Yeshua/Jesus completely into our hearts, then fully we must forgive to function as designed.

Declare: I'm grateful to receive the fullness of Christ's Forgiveness, so I may forgive completely.

"And when you pray, make sure you forgive the faults of others so that your Father in heaven will also forgive you. But if you withhold forgiveness from others, your Father withholds forgiveness from you."

Matthew 6:14-15 TPT

So, just as the heart circulates blood (life) and rejuvenates over and over again, He calls us, for our forgiveness, to forgive over and over again.

Sometimes people may not receive the gift of forgiveness. But your heart will be right when you practice this discipline.

Five minute ACTION:

Forgive. Pray for those you are forgiving. Set your timer and write out anyone who has offended you and bless them with forgiveness. Say "I forgive….."

You may not feel your emotions lining up, but trust the process. Forgive anyway. Say it anyway. Ask Holy Spirit to help you through coaching your emotions to get onboard the ship of Forgiveness.

Quick review:

Rinse and repeat, assume giving and receiving forgiveness is needed. I pray that you use this joy key in life, repeating this daily, for your heart to be soft and ever-ready to let go of bitterness and unforgiveness.

⚜ —·— ⚜

As my mom was in her last days, I was hurt almost daily by unloving behavior and unloving words. In that time, it was a fight to stay in the lane of forgiving, instead of being offended. Today I wonder if I was doing unloving things or saying unloving things, unknowingly provoking offense, which would need forgiveness.

⚜ —·— ⚜

Humbly ask God how to pray to forgive those who offended you and to be forgiven by those you have offended.

Lord, thank you for helping me when I need self-control. Please continue to work a strong ability to hold my thoughts, words, and actions in alignment with Your greater thoughts.

⚜ —·— ⚜

We are designed to forgive. We are made in the image of God. In fact, forgiveness is the Word made flesh, Jesus. So you can read all about it in His Word. Our miraculously loving and just God promises this: Whatever you forgive, to that measure you will be forgiven. Be vigilant to reflect God's forgiveness by forgiving.

⚜ —·— ⚜

Sunshyne Gray, a Christian counselor posted on her website what forgiveness is not. A segment from her list I share here:

⚜ —·— ⚜

"Many think forgiveness somehow excuses or condones the other person's offense.

Not so! Rather, you are entrusting the outcome to God. Putting the consequences of another's sin in the hands of God is a demonstration of obedience and trust in God.

"In your anger do not sin": Do not let the sun go down while you are still angry, and do not give the devil a foothold. -Ephesians 4:26-27

Forgiving is not tolerating.

Forgiving an offense does not mean tolerating behavior that is hurtful. On the contrary, we are called to speak the truth in love (Ephesians 4:15). This is for the good of the offender and the offended. In doing so, we mature as the body of Christ."

Sometimes I remember times when a particular person offended me or did something mean to me or a family member. Old feelings come back, and then I sense Holy Spirit saying to forgive them. I have to make a concentrated effort to yield and bend my will to the Father's. I'm reminded He gave His only Son for me. I ask Him to help me be merciful and understanding. Then suddenly I find myself thinking about what kinds of things may have happened to them to make them so angry and hateful. Then compassion fills my heart for them, and I'm able to pray for them with a pure heart of forgiveness.

L., Clinton, Tennessee

Prayer: Help me remember all the forgiveness I have received for my sins from Christ. Lord, please reveal to me who I need to forgive today. Thank you for designing my heart to give and receive forgiveness.

Hope, Joy, and Peace are the fruits of a detoxed heart, free of bitterness and unforgiveness. Amen.

Five-minute ACTION:

Write a thank you note to God in your journal today, He has forgiven you 100%. Not 99.9%. Let that sink in – fully.

Michael Koulianos[3] had the privilege to review Katherine Kuhlman's letters to God in her journal with his father in law. She would start her letters, "My dearest Jesus".

Jesus is the Word made flesh. The greatest gift of all time. Lord, let my life be a thank you for Your great gift.

Joy Key: Forgive.

3.*https://youtu.be/SNKgUE_ztfA*

11. Savor Savior – Chocolate Meditation

To savor God, lets being by practicing savoring. It also aligns with thinking deeply to hear God, slowing down and inviting unplanned divine appointments to enter in.

I am learning to savor food. It is my life-long journey. I have a history of eating fast. Under the blood of Jesus, Lord has helped me slow down…some.

A sidebar, (not a distraction) – An article in The Epoch Times sited the following: Chewing thoroughly is associated with less pain and better brain function. Please stay away from processed sugar for better health. Before you close this book mumbling 'buzz kill,' consider taking a seven-day fast from processed foods and sugar. After 7 days, see how you feel. I learned and re-learned a little sugar goes a long way toward yucky inflammation. Though there is a brief energy boost with sugar, it is hard on your system.

I shared this meditation when on chocolate it received many comments on social media, so I am sharing it here. Dark chocolate doesn't have much sugar.

You can also use fresh organic strawberries or another sweet fruit, like peaches.

The sweet Power of the Savor…to know abundance without overindulgence.

Chocolate Meditation

Choose some chocolate - either a type that you've never tried before or one that you have not eaten recently. It might be dark and flavorsome, organic, fair-trade - or cheap and trashy.

The important thing is to choose a type you wouldn't normally eat or that you consume only rarely.

Here goes:

• Open the packet. Inhale the aroma. Let it sweep over you.

• Break off a piece and look at it. Really let your eyes drink in what it looks like, examining every nook and cranny.

• Pop it in your mouth. See if it is possible to hold it on your tongue and let it melt, noticing any tendency to suck on it. Chocolate has over 300 different flavors. See if you can sense some of them.

• If you notice your mind wandering while you do this, simply notice where it went, then gently escort it back to the present moment.

• After the chocolate has completely melted, swallow it very slowly and deliberately. Let it trickle down your throat.

• Repeat this with one other piece.

Now, consider cherishing and dreaming of more savoring moments with God, family & friends.

Like a treasure hunt, look for the Jesus you see in others.

I confess, I got behind! But each daily devotional is such a refreshing drink of water! I find my time here in the 21-day Journey to be both precious and blessed. Holy Spirit tells me to sing more, pray evermore, and to remember that Jesus is on his way back to the earth and we are to be ready. I love that you wrote your words on the bedroom mirror. I did too!—E., Alabama

JOY Key: Savor life - enJoy every season.

12. Superpower: Pearl Maker

Have you ever been agitated by someone? A shift in perspective. What if we look at agitation as an opportunity to create a pearl with God in prayer? By praying and seeking God, He can shift things and cover you and the agitator with His view. Redemption for the agitation.

Prayer: a superpower to make pearls.

Pray for your family. Declare God's promises over your children and pray those over them. A pearl is formed when an oyster is agitated. What if we join His promise to see all things working for good for those who love Him? (Romans 8:28). So now, instead of focus on problems, pray and see these as your pearls to be. Ahhh…your heart may see an enemy, a source of pain, but God sees a way to make a pearl for you and place it in the throne room of your heart. This pearl-making strategy is the divine wisdom of God. He has a way of changing perspective.

Journal your insights, glory promises over problems.

Be a Pearl Maker

⤋⤋⤋⤋

I've been worrying a lot lately and I remember an exercise we did a long time ago when I was in church overseas. We did daily faith confessions. We wrote down scriptures to renew our mind with God's word and recited them daily and every time we met before Bible study. You would stand up and share one you memorized that you needed at that time in your life. As you talk about God's promises, I'm reminded I need to write down a few promises of the many and recite them daily. As you are teaching us our thoughts become words and our words actions, I need to speak to that worry in me, the fear of the future and so forth, and start declaring God's Word daily over me again so that party in my head will stop and Philippians 4:8 will take over. Sometimes it's a matter of taking that armor of God, dusting it off and putting it on all over again because life happens. We get tired and we forget who we are and who we belong to.

N., Huntsville, AL

You may already have noticed that everything is interrelated. As we detox our thoughts, our words will change. As our words change, our actions will often change, too. We are making small, (maybe 1%?) changes over and over again, to gain a gain, again and again.

I encourage you to pray for, and believe in, family reconciliation. I pray faith, hope, and love over each prayer on your hearts to believe and see family reconciliation until the prayers are answered.

When I was writing the negativity fast/Toxic Thought Detox, we named it,

Journey to Joy: a 21-Day Thought Detox. In that time, I was taken to Isaiah

55:

"For my thoughts are not your thoughts, neither are your ways my ways,"
declares the LORD.
As the heavens are higher than the earth, so are my ways higher than your
ways and my thoughts than your thoughts."

Isaiah 55 : 8-9 NIV

When my mom was in her last days, I felt the Lord prepare me to die to

self while I watched my mother die. He was so close during those days.

Within this time of grieving, another family member was hurting too,

and would say words that hurt my heart. At almost every word spoken

my heart was wounded. I repented for not praying more passionately

for the healing of this one wounding my heart. I realized where there

was offense, there was pride. God called me to pray passionately and die

to self, to the pride in me. It was hard. I felt offended. As I passionately

prayed, I witnessed the dial move to God's better way. God touched

the offender and the offended. Hearts were made tender, not perfect,

but able to navigate the season with flashes of love and kindness. I

understood the wisdom in proverbs.

> *"The path of the virtuous leads away from evil;*
> *whoever follows that path is safe.*
> *Pride goes before destruction,*
> *and haughtiness before a fall.*
> *Better to live humbly with the poor*
> *than to share plunder with the proud.*
> *Those who listen to instruction will prosper;*
> *those who trust the Lord will be joyful.*
> *The wise are known for their understanding,*
> *and pleasant words are persuasive.*

Proverbs 16:17-21 NLT

God wants us in intimacy with Him to discern what is truly important. Our thoughts impact our heart posture. This heart posture not only impacts our words, but the way we say them. Have you ever heard, "You're just saying that"? A God-centered heart posture as we say our words impacts our family and how we live our life with all our relationships.

Remember the shift in perspective to be a pearl maker? You are a precious child of God, co-creating beauty from pain, changing the atmosphere in this renewal process.

Our thoughts agreeing with God's thoughts are like the oyster's nacre making a pearl. With a humble heart, you are more likely to have compassion and mercy to work things out. God gives us the right heart posture in prayer. I know I have unintentionally offended or irritated others in the past. I pray they can forgive me.

For + Give = Pearls of Love and Wisdom

Today, I will continue to seek God's perspective on all life matters.

"How truly wonderful and delightful
to see brothers and sisters living together in sweet unity!
It's as precious as the sacred scented oil
flowing from the head of the high priest Aaron,
dripping down upon his beard and running all the way down
to the hem of his priestly robes.
This heavenly harmony can be compared to the dew
dripping down from the skies upon Mount Hermon,
refreshing the mountain slopes of Israel.
For from this realm of sweet harmony
God will release his eternal blessing, the promise of life forever!"

Psalm 133 TPT

We are amalgamated into spirit and truth by His word and our testimony.

At the end of life, we will stand alone before God.

Did I demonstrate living in Spirit and Truth? This is our life in Christ. We are all connected in the body of Christ. God wants us to be known by our harmony and love. Let us pray we can carry the power of this to the world.

Five minute ACTION:

Sit with your journal in a quiet time and breath the healing belly breath. Read Psalm 133 and Isaiah 55.

A longer Action: After you have read these verses, set your timer for 10 minutes. This may sound weird or morbid, but I thank Steve Witt for this exercise which fueled me many years ago. I am asking you to write your obituary. Write it as you would like to have completed your life. Write it as you finished well. Imagine God's plans and what they would look like fulfilled in your life. Go Big. I took longer on this, maybe half an hour. Steve asked a few volunteers to read their obituaries at this leadership event. I volunteered. Several told me that they felt the spirit of the Lord was on the words I declared for the end of my life. I keep this obituary close to my heart. It encourages me to keep going in my daily 1% moves to be more like our Lord designed me to be.

I was so blessed by the devotional on family reconciliation. This is something that has been on my heart for a long time!! Your prayer in the video blessed me so much and after journaling and reading the Scriptures, I am filled with hope and faith to gain a gain again and again!!! Amen!! -U., Ohio

Joy Key: Cover life's agitation with prayer –

Be a Pearl Maker

13. Kind Actions

Have you ever received a random act of kindness?

We had just gotten my 92-year-old mom out of the hospital. Max, my oldest son, was about to leave Alabama to live with his brother in California for a few months. My dad wanted to take us to dinner to celebrate his Bon voyage and our Alabama family together. Our Alabama clan is a tall, eclectic company, representing three generations, three white hairs coming in around 6 feet and young Max at 6' 7". When we arrived at a local steak restaurant, we had a bit of a struggle getting mom to the table. Max, the young pioneer about to head west, had mostly carried mom to the table in her weakened state. As we were settling in, I noticed a couple at a table adjacent to our booth. Our eyes met, we smiled. I didn't think another thing about it.

The couple rose to go and came up to our table. Smiling at mom first, then the rest of us, the man spoke, "How is everybody doing? I would like to buy you all dessert tonight." He placed a folded bill under his hand and continued a few more words of kindness, for us to enjoy our meal, and dessert was on him. We thanked him, and they left us there, surprised and blessed by their generosity. Stunned etiquette kept that bill folded as my dad told my son to take this gift with him to California. Grateful Max obediently took the bill and put it in his pocket. We chatted a bit about the kindness of the couple and then my curiosity rose up. I asked, "Max, how much did he give you?" (Truly expecting this generous gift to be a $10 or $20 dollar bill.) Max responded he didn't check. He then reached into his pocket and unfolded the bill on the table. It was a $100 bill! SLAP. What? Yes, that sneaky generous guy had hit us with a HUGE gift under the guise of 'buying our dessert'. For me, seeing our family be the recipient of something spectacular like that…I am activated to think of ways to 'pay it forward'.   Imagine a waitress getting that as a surprise tip?

Are you ready to take action? You can start with family and friends or enjoy this powerful fun with complete strangers. Kindness rules are pretty simple. Practice kindness for the practice. Practice, practice, practice, with zero expectations or obligations to receive a kindness in return. Sometimes receivers are grateful, sometimes stunned, sometimes suspicious. This is about sharing the goodness of God and practicing intimacy with God in every moment. The idea is about making it a habit. It joins the other keys for life. Ask God how you can do this Joy key.

Pray about what you could do to bless someone else. You may get a very specific thing, or a general thing. My Ohio friend, Linda, packs food/

toiletries in bundles to hand out to the homeless. I believe she must have earned most every heavenly scout preparedness badge. I admire her forethought. Is there joy in your heart when you receive an idea? Bless someone with it!

In 2020, I read our U.S. Postal system was on the brink of closing. What about mailing someone a card? Buy some cool stamps. That is some preparing…I think Linda is having an influence on me. May you be twice blessed as you bless others.

Declaration

"Perfect, absolute peace surrounds those whose imaginations are consumed with you; they confidently trust in you."

Isaiah 26:3

Prayer: Lord, will you share your divine inspiration for fun ways to bless other people? Please give me insight, partnerships, resources and zeal to complete the acts of kindness. Lord, I love to partner with you to bless others with acts of kindness.

Joy Key: Random Acts of Kindness.

14. Worship in Life

"Problems cannot be solved with the same mindset that created them."

Albert Einstein

Confession time: I hum and sing as I'm shopping for groceries. I am tuning to God as I hum. This key has opened doors to some people coming up to me to thank me. One man said it reawakened him to sing while shopping, too. My heart is different when I am praising. It changes my thought patterns, as well.

We are designed to worship.

Worship tunes thoughts to what is truly important.

I am focused on His peace in my assignment.

Communing with Holy Spirit, I can remember what is needed, and for help selecting the best produce. Holy Spirit knows a good melon…I'm just saying.

Maybe there's a whistle in you if you're not a singer. What simple change do you want to start to worship as you live?

And now a word from Saint Paul:

"Let every activity of your lives and every word that comes from your lips be drenched with the beauty of our Lord Jesus, the Anointed One. And bring your constant praise to God the Father because of what Christ has done for you!"

Colossians 3:18 TPT

Ten Minute ACTION:

Take 10 minutes to pause, breathe, and MOVE with God.

Set your timer for 10 minutes, hide your phone, and remember the belly breath of healing. Declare your three simple powerful words. As you enter this time, know you are entering into an agreement with Jesus as you seek to hear from God.

You can stretch. You can dance. You can walk. You can vacuum. Just welcome Holy Spirit to do these and all things with you.

"Proverbs 10:22, 'The blessing of the Lord makes a person rich, and he adds no sorrow with it', stood out to me today. I started thinking about these words, blessings of the Lord, and recalled how He saved me from my destructive path. Then I studied rich. Of course, financial comes to mind first, but I looked up the definition of the word and it has so much more attached to it. When I considered all the other meanings and pondered the way God fulfills those definitions, joy started to bubble up in my heart. Joy! Then I thought of you and how your devotionals are focusing on Joy! I say this to encourage you to keep going, you're on the right track.

—T., Huntsville, Alabama

Highlighted in this verse is, "he adds no sorrow." During COVID, my friend Victoria and her fiancé Rex, now husband, hosted a Seder meal via Zoom. While we reflected on the elements of the Sedar meal, salt water was there to recall the tears in Exodus. God's purpose then and now is to set the captives free. Be it from persecution, or from our own toxic thoughts, He is the one with the keys to freedom. Praise Jesus! His plans are to set us free so we can run to His open arms with grateful hearts to receive His powerful love and eternal joy! I pray you are strengthened with His abundant joy right now.

Joy Key: Worship Him in all you do.

15. Rest

Sabbath. In Hebrew tradition, there is a day of rest to be with family and God. To enter a day of rest is holy. It is a choice. This tradition is not what we see in our culture.

You may already take a day of rest or you may feel it is impossible.

Several years ago, I had an intense wake up call to rest.

In that season I was an IT manager and a recovering workaholic. While better than my earlier days, I was still missing opportunities to savor life.

My wakeup call occurred on a cold January morning. Walking my dog over a wintry terrain at 4:30 am., in the early dark cold, I wasn't fully present, instead I was thinking of all I needed to do that day. Rushing through this mundane task to go to the next thing, I slipped on black ice and broke my ankle…in two places. A titanium plate was installed in my right leg to commemorate the occasion. Many weeks of forced rest followed. So there was my wake-up call to surrender to be more present and seek God in all things. Denying rest to go, go, go… may appear to work for a while, but it is stealing simple joys, and with it, life itself. Killjoy time. It will deplete you of joy.

When I allow a day of rest and slow down, in general, I welcome peace into my thoughts, words and actions.

During my forced rest I fasted and prayed. This wasn't just a holy thing, though. I also didn't want to gain weight for many weeks while I was recovering and couldn't walk.

A side note: I chose to make and drink cucumber smoothies. I discovered many of cucumbers health benefits, most notably, cucumbers are a powerful diuretic. Not being able to walk necessitated unusual acrobatic adventures to and from the bathroom during my recovery.

As you attempt remove that image from your sanctified imagination, I would like to share how God used these days of rest.

It was in this time I sought deeper joy keys to life. Breathing, savoring simple joys and more keys as I rested with God.

At that time, I had been a corporate comedian on a talent booking agency site for about six years. I stopped taking gigs when I was promoted to IT Manager for an Ohio insurance company. Several leaders at that company had asked me to share the talk I had delivered to the Human Resources group, to their divisions. This talk I felt was my life in a message.

As I rested and healed, I did research on detoxing from toxic thinking. I prepared a revised message to share more joy keys when I was back on my feet.

I changed categories on the agent website from comedian to motivational speaker. I listed Resilience as my talk, and in the description something about keys for more joy and less stress. I prayed all Psalm 136.

I share v.1, 23-26 verses (NIV) here:

"Give thanks to the Lord, for he is good.
His love endures forever.
He remembered us in our low estate,
His love endures forever.
and freed us from our enemies.
His love endures forever.
He gives food to every creature.
His love endures forever.
Give thanks to the God of heaven.
His love endures forever."

I was booked for 3 events in 3 different states in as many days. I remember trying to say no to one event planner, because I didn't have time to drive from Berea Kentucky to Detroit Michigan the next morning. The Berea College event planner changed their event time so I could speak there.

God wanted to get this message out.

Grateful. I met some amazing people in Berea Kentucky. A year later I received the agency's award for Best Motivational Speaker. All this is to say, God used this time to teach me about the fruit of spending time with Him.

We are designed to have intermittent rests. Every week, every day, every hour, we can rest in Him, and find sabbath. We are created in His image and He took a day of rest, remember?

Closer than eyelashes, He is wanting to provide comfort, wisdom, peace, and joy in His presence.

"As we enter into God's faith-rest life, we cease from our own works. Just as God celebrates His finished works and rests in them. So, then we must give our all and be eager to experience this faith-rest life so that no one falls short by following the same pattern of doubt and unbelief."

Hebrews 4:10-11 TPT

Because of Yeshua/Jesus, we can rest in Him every day. Devoting a day to reflect, relax, and have focused time with family and friends, makes it a joy to trust Abba with our sabbath. When we honor this, we honor our original design.

Resting is a great way to reboot and reclaim hope stolen by the enemy of life.

During our 21-day devotional, I interviewed my friend Joy about how she detoxes her thoughts. The video is available (as of this writing) with others from the devotional days @DawnofResilience on YouTube. She shared how she speaks His word over situations that might provoke worry or fear. This disciplines her to rest in His word and not toxic worry.

Power of Words

> *"Perfect, absolute peace surrounds those whose imaginations are consumed with you; they confidently trust in you."*

> *Isaiah 26:3*

A day of Rest = ACTION:

Take a day to pause and breathe and rest in God's Word. Practice listening well to the ones you see. What is God saying through their words and actions? What would be your life scripture?

As you enter this time, practice joy keys as you enter into agreement with His promises. Let Him continue to heal the hidden hurts as you reflect on His Word for you.

Remember the Sabbath day by keeping it holy. Six days you shall labor and do all your work, but the seventh day is a sabbath to the Lord your God. On it you shall not do any work, neither you, nor your son or daughter, nor your male or female servant, nor your animals, nor any foreigner residing in your towns.

Exodus 20:8-10

My Ohio pastor and friend, **James Baker**[1], had a dream where he saw Abba in the word Sabbath. Sabbath, a day of rest. Rest in Him and meet with him in the day of rest.

Trusting God with your time is a love offering. Here's your invitation to 'Just do it'.

The Hebrew day begins at sunset. That kind of gives a different perspective on the expression 'Don't let the sun set on your anger...' (Eph. 4:26-27).

1.https://www.wealthwithgod.com/

If your day begins at night, you wouldn't want to start the day being angry, would you?

In Hebrew tradition, the day of rest is celebrated. Ever hear 'Shabbat Shalom!'? It is a day of rest. It begins at sunset Friday night and concludes Saturday at sunset. A family meal begins this traditional day of rest.

Declaration:

"I will continue to seek a healthy REST in faith in all my life matters."

My new third word this session is 'Champion'. It reflects my heart's desire to fight for righteousness. Before doing the dream assignment on Day 7, I went back and reviewed the last session's dream page that I wrote, thinking I had recorded all my heart's desires. But on Day 7 this time, God downloaded the very dreams of my heart that just might see my desire to be a 'Champion' fulfilled!—M., Colorado Springs, CO

Joy Key: Rest with Him in a sABBAth.

16. Your Story's Author

"You cannot keep birds from flying over your head

but you can keep them from building a nest in your hair"

Martin Luther

Your thoughts, words, and actions are writing your life story. Emotions are powerful, they are not safe drivers for your life story.

Emotions can be delightful accompaniments in their role to magnify life. This is a life God gave us, with an invitation to write our story with Him. A life to worship Him in awe, to passionately pray, with freedom to choose God's keys to a life in abundant joy.

What is your story saying? In 2020 during the Easter season, I watched the Passion of Christ with my oldest. It was the first time Max had seen the film. I wonder how God is using this film to impact those who have seen it. It touched me. So has The Chosen, a crowd funded production which brings the Word to life.

As I write, I don't know the fullness of the impact, but I believe anyone who experiences God's pure love is forever changed. I believe the entertainment industry can be used by God to bring more closer to Him.

Intimacy with God deepens wisdom and joy. Taking communion daily brings me to deeper and deeper gratitude for Jesus, His life and sacrifice, the greatest gift ever.

When we keep meditating on the vast goodness of God, we gain confidence in His truth. His truth trumps our toxic perspective of a situation. This one key changes the trajectory of our life story.

I heard someone say, "When we worry, we are putting our faith in the wrong kingdom."

Don't copy the behavior and customs of this world, but let God transform you into a new person by changing the way you think. Then you will learn to know God's will for you, which is good and pleasing and perfect.

Romans 12:2 NLT

Our author and finisher has a better word. I want to partner with God's plans and purposes. Communing with Him brings deep joy as I go about the tasks, projects, and work. Keep Him first and He will make a way.

Casting down imaginations, and every high thing that exalteth itself against the knowledge of God, and bringing into captivity every thought to the obedience of Christ.

2 Corinthians 10:5 KJV

Power of Thoughts

What are vain imaginations? Imagining without God.

When I imagine with God, I am seeking His view. God sees all things. He understands all things. He promises all things will work together for good as we love Him, we enter the call of His purpose. As I trust God, He will provide more answers than I could imagine.

～ഒ ———— ഒ～

Perfect, absolute peace surrounds those whose imaginations are consumed with you; they confidently trust in you.

Isaiah 26:3

～ഒ ———— ഒ～

So grateful you are making journaling part of our action assignments. My thoughts and my daily routine can be like a butterfly flitting from one lovely flower to the next.....but when I stop to write in my journal, then I really pause long enough to breathe and go deeper in my own thoughts and heart—and His!! —C, Huntsville, Alabama

～ഒ ———— ഒ～

So, we are convinced that every detail of our lives is continually woven together to fit into God's perfect plan of bringing good into our lives, for we are his lovers who have been called to fulfill his designed purpose.

Romans 8:28 TPT

～ഒ ———— ഒ～

10 Minute Action:

Take 10 minutes to pause, breathe, and rest in God's Word. Read Romans 8:9-30 out loud. With your journal in hand, set your timer for 10 minutes. Breathe the healing belly breath. Declare your three simple powerful words. As you enter this time, know you are entering into agreement with a higher way with Yeshua/Jesus, as you seek to hear from Him. Let Him speak to you about today, about making pearls from hidden hurts, to heal sickness, to have a 1% action for a dream, pray to release any toxic thoughts as you breathe, reflecting on His word, write a letter to God.

I have a testimony about my dream page. I had a dream for my next mission trip. I put down a time, and a place I believed the Lord was showing me. Then last night I thought about my mission dream again and started asking the Lord about a missionary family I would like to go with. I was just talking to the Lord about this mission trip on my dream page and who I want to go with. Today (after not hearing from this girl for two years) she contacted me! I had been on a mission trip with her before. She said that the Lord brought me to her mind last night. That's when I was asking the Lord about her and her family for this dream mission!!! I told her about writing this on my dream page, and she was so excited. We were praying for each other at the same time!!

– M., Frankfort, OH

Joy Key: Think like God - All Things are Possible

17. Harvest & Habits

It is early spring, a beautiful, crisp day. I love to make soup and stew, especially when it's chilly outside. Today I had chicken and vegetable soup. As my brain and my body team up to let go of the extra weight put on between 2020 and now, I am learning to move around after my meal. Little lifestyle changes. It started with increasing activity and drinking enough water. New habits are kind of like seeds. The thought seed of a new habit needs to germinate, grow roots, and then establish itself. The science behind habits is in the camp of behavioral psychology. Or as I consider it, brain gardening.

I am forming healthy habits so I can enjoy food while I lose weight. The habits of a healthy person are key to reaching the weight I have set as 'the goal'. In another chapter I shared a small changes journey of a woman who started making decisions by asking, 'What would a healthy person do?' Over a period of time, the decisions she made formed her healthy habits and she lost over 100 pounds. At the beginning of her becoming, she identified with "I am healthy" as a goal. Her decisions created habits which led her to be the healthy person she set out to be. We can practice habits into our Christ identity. I am tapping into visualizing myself as a lighter person now, and even though there is more downward movement needed on the scale to align my goal weight, I am sowing into this future now.

As we tap into our identity in Christ, we realize God has more than we can fathom for us. Born again makes you a special breed. You are called courageous before you feel courageous. You are called victorious before you see a victory. You are called to do the impossible because Christ lives in you. Remember these three words:

Faith pleases God.

I live, pray and worship up on Monte Sano. Monte Sano a Spanish phrase meaning mountain of health. Back to that cool spring afternoon, I had just finished lunch and am walking my dog, Pepper. In the spring coolness, the bugs and vegetation seem to rest under the leaves of last fall. I feel Holy Spirit calling me to trust Him and to do an uncharted thing. Walking Pepper to the end of the cul-de-sac, I follow His prompting.

I know He wants to meet with me in a place I am to discover. The goal is to descend the tree filled steep incline of the mountain to the valley carrying the mountain stream of one of Monte Sano's waterfalls. Carefully Pepper and I descend. The leaves are thick on the ground. Finding each step's footing as we zig zag through fallen limbs and trees with the sun dappling the ground before us. I am praying in spirit, checking each step, holding onto saplings for support as my leashed faithful dog and I go lower and lower. At fallen trees and rocks, I say "jump" to Pepper, so as not to tangle his leash on the many young trees. I feel God with us, so I am not afraid, but I am watching every single step, thoughtful, as we make our path down. The rocks of the mountain stream meet us at the water's edge. There is a clearing near the rocks. To me, it is a rejoicing sound of water over rocks, congratulating us for the successful descent. A large flat stone with a smaller 'sitting stone' is waiting for us. Stepping stone to stone, we meet Him, as the sun is warming us. I feel His presence. We are in a personal sanctuary. There we sit to meet His beauty. A large crystal-clear pool with sand-covered stones is before me as Pepper lays resting at my feet. Above it the mountain's spring is pouring down with its song.

I am overcome with joy, faith steps into victory to be with Him and the beauty before me.

Fear would have kept me away. Fear would say don't go, you 62-year-old woman with a plate in your leg. Don't you dare. But God was with me. Faith said go with my dog down that Monte Sano incline.

In our waterfront sanctuary I immediately know in my spirit to release Psalm 139 out loud.

As you read Psalm 139, consider your toxic thoughts the 'enemies' and 'murderers'. Aren't they? They destroy hope and dreams, faith and wisdom and your ability to walk in your true strength as a child of God.

"O Lord, you have examined my heart and know everything about me.

You know when I sit down or stand up.

You know my thoughts even when I'm far away.

You see me when I travel and when I rest at home.

You know everything I do. You know what I am going to say even before I say it, Lord.

You go before me and follow me. You place your hand of blessing on my head.

Such knowledge is too wonderful for me, too great for me to understand!

I can never escape from your Spirit! I can never get away from your presence!

If I go up to heaven, you are there; if I go down to the grave, you are there.

If I ride the wings of the morning, if I dwell by the farthest oceans, even there your hand will guide me, and your strength will support me.

I could ask the darkness to hide me and the light around me to become night—but even in darkness I cannot hide from you.

To you the night shines as bright as day. Darkness and light are the same to you.

You made all the delicate, inner parts of my body and knit me together in my mother's womb.

Thank you for making me so wonderfully complex!

Your workmanship is marvelous—how well I know it.

You watched me as I was being formed in utter seclusion, as I was woven together in the dark of the womb.

You saw me before I was born. Every day of my life was recorded in your book.

Every moment was laid out before a single day had passed.

How precious are your thoughts about me, O God.

They cannot be numbered!

I can't even count them; they outnumber the grains of sand! And when I wake up, you are still with me!

O God, if only you would destroy the wicked!

Get out of my life, you murderers!

They blaspheme you; your enemies misuse your name.

O Lord, shouldn't I hate those who hate you? Shouldn't I despise those who oppose you?

Yes, I hate them with total hatred, for your enemies are my enemies.

Search me, O God, and know my heart; test me and know my anxious thoughts.

Point out anything in me that offends you, and lead me along the path of everlasting life."

Ps. 139 NLT

Then I prayed. After the precious meeting, Pepper and I made our way to the street near the creek, and met some new neighbors as we ascended a steep street I have renamed from suicide to 'Overcomers Hill' on the way to our home. I had prayed to meet neighbors. God answered.

As you champion your thoughts to align with God's thoughts for you, it will transform your outlook and ultimately your life. Your story is unique and powerful when touched by the blood of Yeshua/Jesus. I have grown more and more in love with how God sees his children. We are surrounded by champions.

Earlier in the book there was a testimony of 'M', a subscriber who picked a new word. 'I am a Champion'. Remember the Queen song "We are the Champions?" Recently, (August 2023) Dolly Parton released **a new version of We are the Champions w/We will rock you**[1]. I listened to it a couple of times. It feels like Dolly is offering an invitation to awaken the champion spirit inside each of us. Could Dolly be calling us to live with a blood-bought backbone? To prepare the way of the Lord? You may think me a little wonky for looking at Dolly's song as prophetic. But God speaks to us in many ways. Earlier in the year, Dolly released **another single in 2023**[2] where she sings of a dream she had where God was saying 'don't make me have to come down there'. That song is a call for us to wake up and live right.

____

1. *https://youtu.be/4UYtJUYrGQQ*
2. *https://youtu.be/UQmX7jT2LEg*

We are Champions with God

I accept the divine invitation to wake up and activate my true design. Do you? We are more than conquerors, to see great transformations for family, community, our nation, and anyone in our sphere of influence who needs an intimate relationship with Yeshua/Jesus.

Breathe in and declare God's view of you – I am a champion. Invest time with Him for great joy through renewing your mind.

We're in this together.

I hope you find this book transformational.   In the time I was Jo Ann's faith 'person' during her seven-year battle with cancer, I took it as my battle, too. I hurt so much when her body quit working. But God met me in worship and let me know with His great love, she would see His throne room before me. This ministered to my heart to let her go when she went home.

With my son's mental breakdown, the enemy crossed the family line. It was WAR, and God brought several powerful intercessors into the battle with me. I am forever grateful.

My mother's illness and death, followed by my sons' paternal grandmother illness and death ten days later, left our family walking tenderly, as we knew each of us were hurting and grieving. Yet, because Emmanuel, 'God with us' is ever present, He led me, like the descent on the mountain that day with Pepper, through the many steps and challenges of grieving. With every little 'irk' of life, God is ready to capture your heart like a lover saying 'Don't look there, look at ME.''

Our country and the world is in a mental health crisis.

I pray God's joy keys lift you, strengthen you and keep you going. Then you can spread His light, too.

We give thanks. That is to say, our family prays over our meals. When the boys were younger, we prayed for the faith of superheroes. Now we often give thanks and ask for the faith of Shadrach, Meshack and Abednego. The latter was most likely inspired when my fried green tomatoes set off the fire alarm. Whatever the case, I invite you to say grace over your meals at home and in restaurants.

Give thanks in all circumstances.

Take Five x3 ACTION:

I invite you to take 10 – 15 minutes to do something toward your health. If you are able, take a walk. Activate your imagination and bless your body parts with God's healing. Or, if you cannot walk, lay or sit and bless your body for His healing. Give thanks and consider what 1% you can do toward your dreams or your health. When we are grateful, we create expectancy for the more, we bless the not enough in faith, with a grateful heart. God can multiply a grateful heart's desire to more than enough. Think of the little fish and loaves that our dear Yeshua gave thanks over, to see the not enough multiply to feed thousands. Give thanks for the seeds of your dreams. Water them and believe Him as you stretch into bigger faith for God to provide a way for the more.

Remember your three simple "I am…" words? As you enter this timed session, know you are entering into agreement with Jesus for your health. Thank God for all the parts of your body and bless all the parts, especially those in need to be healed. Stretch, dance, or take a short walk if you're able. When the timer goes off, give thanks.

> Loved and grabbed onto this from today's devotion:
> When we agree with His view of us, with His
> overflowing love for us, we gain confidence in His truth.
>
> L., Grove City, Ohio

Joy Key: Give Thanks in ALL circumstances. Thes. 5:18

18. Listen & Learn

Quality listening begins by practicing listening to God. His Word provides His tuning for peace, wisdom and joy.

Listening to others allows me to seek, like a scavenger hunt, the gold Jesus has put in people.

The state motto of Ohio is "With God all things are possible."

I like the idea of taking on the impossible with God. I like hanging out with people who also embrace this ideal. One of my mentors is a visionary. She stirs me to stretch my belief into the more with God. I am fueled by her victories, to stretch me in business and life, and go to greater heights with God.

On the other hand, if I give up, quit seeking His direction, am I not forsaking Him? I recently heard Ken Fish(a biblical scholar, and honors graduate of Princeton University) say we have been shutting God out of our society for at least thirty years. Yikes. Time for reflection.

Ask yourself if you have felt joy has left you? Have you felt God has forsaken you? Ask yourself, when did I forsake God?

Repent. Reboot. And begin afresh today. Ask for a fresh perspective to connect with your Creator. Go back to gratitude for breath, simple joys, identity words, in the beginning chapters, or the Field of Dreams chapter. Dream again. Ask other people about their dreams. Consider dreaming and doing with God and with others.

I believe listening is a life-long skill to practice. Both listening to God and listening to others. Time set apart to hear God's plan for your life and time to be open to align with others to contribute to His big picture.

As you invest in these little actions, you are growing deeper roots to unlock more joy. Keep going and growing. We're on the home stretch!

A by-product of listening well, is growing stronger relationships. When people feel heard, love grows, relationships mature and compassion for fellow man grows to strengthen family and all relationships.

In our world, I know there are those who are toxic, endangering themselves and others. With these we take appropriate boundaries.

We all need God.

Fasting and prayer are powerful tools, as we pray for those who are oppressed in harmful behavior.

Todd White was a lost and 'bad dude' until he was found. He was prayed over, ministered to, and redeemed. For the last 19 years he has prayed, discipled and led others to God most every day. Cindy Jacobs interviewed him in 2023. It is available on YouTube, if you would like to hear his testimony.

126

Prayer

My dear Jesus, please touch the unlovable with your love. Please bring radical prayer and believers to pour out on each of them to radically save them, as you did Todd White. Amen.

I have seen toxic relationships restored to healthy thriving relationships. If you are uncertain how to navigate your relationship dynamic, find someone with integrity and compassion to help you on the road to healing and forgiveness. Seek God first, then He will guide you.

Somewhere along the way I learned this BIG life lesson.

Nobody is perfect.

According to my dad this was my mantra when I was little. I would hear my parents calling out the faults they saw in me. They meant for me to improve. Deep down in me, though, I developed a belief I wasn't good enough to be loved if I made mistakes. Seeing my life through the lens of conditional love was stressful. A lie from satan, for sure.

Mom set high standards. She was beautiful, smart, hard-working, and doors opened for her to do things which seemed impossible. Dad, too, was accomplished, pioneering guidance and navigation to the moon with NASA on Apollo.

I allowed the critical spirit into my life in those early years.

God's love is patient and kind, unconditional and encouraging.

Partnering with God, over time, I adapted to see the joy in the journey to excellence. This is different than the torturing critic, seeing myself as 'not good enough' comparing myself to some impossible perfection. Willing to do new things imperfectly as God led me to step into new things with Him.

He already did the work, and I can be at peace as I pour passion into my practice in life.

During my school years I competed in acting, debate and speech (to name a few). I worked to perfect my character and my message. I enjoyed the work. The practice is part of the process. To do this, is to be in the key of joy in the process. This along with His eternal wisdom: It's okay to try and fail. Peace during progress. That's how we learn. Sweet self-forgiveness. This is how God wants us to be. It is a key to abundant joy. Whether you're a golfer, gymnast, swimmer, dancer, athlete, or a working mom perfecting sourdough bread and meatloaf, I praise your discipline to a joyful passion to excellence in your process. I invite you to be a hope carrier to others. As we learn self-forgiveness, perhaps the grace and forgiveness God has called us to impart will become possible. Not perfect, just trained on a hope-filled future. Choose to look for opportunities to be a hope carrier and carry hope with passion and purpose.

My mom was 92 when she bent to sit on a chair in a restaurant. She slipped, fell to the floor, and fractured her hip. She didn't walk again. Two months after the accident, mom was back with dad in their independent living apartment. My oldest son, Max, rose to serve his grandparents. I had a speaking engagement in Ohio and was gone for a week during this time. Max helped my dad lift and care for mom. When I came home to this scene, I was moved by the heroic character demonstrated in my son's actions. He was a hub for hospice and a primary caregiver to mom her last months with us. This same son who had faced chronic depression and a suicide attempt in 2021 was now a mighty hero for our family. He was a loving connection between family and hospice care. Max means greatest. The way he cares for others is in his name.

Much like the spring flowers say yes, winter is over and there will be a harvest soon, we can catch and release the 'yes and amen' hope of God. Consider what you can do to make a bright spot in the day. I trust you and God will come up with a perfect way to provide a little bright spot of hope in someone else's day.

God sees us as mighty oaks.

❧ — ❧

'and provide for those who grieve in Zion—to bestow on them a crown of beauty instead of ashes, the oil of joy instead of mourning, and a garment of praise instead of a spirit of despair. They will be called oaks of righteousness, a planting of the Lord for the display of His splendor.'

Is. 61:3

There are 22 varieties of oak in Alabama, the 22nd state in the nation.

May we all be righteous, and a display of His splendor.

❧ — ❧

Nevertheless, I will bring health and healing to it, I will heal my people and will let them enjoy abundant peace and security.

Jeremiah 33:6 NLT

❧ — ❧

We are interwoven together, to honor God and support each other for a greater purpose.

Declare: Jesus intercedes for me. Jesus intercedes for us.

He is able to save fully, from now throughout eternity, everyone who comes to God through him, because he lives to pray continually for them.

Hebrews 7:25 TPT

Declaration:

I know my God and I trust HIM. He loves me seeing Him in this love light. Jesus is praying for me all the time. I know ("I am...." your three words) I am ___, I am ___, I am ____. I am in love with the author of love and He provides all my needs.

Declaration of His Word: God is able to bless me abundantly, so that in all things, at all times, having all that I need, I will abound in every good work.

2 Corinthians 9:8 (revised pronouns you to me/I for declaration)

The Lord is good, a stronghold in the day of trouble; and He knows those who trust in Him.

Nahum 1:7

Five-minute ACTION:

"Look at the birds of the air; they do not sow or reap or store away in barns, and yet your heavenly Father feeds them. Are you not much more valuable than they? Can any one of you by worrying add a single hour to your life?!

Luke 12:26-27 NIV

(If you can, get a bird feeder. It could be another joy key.)

Today's action – Find a short scripture verse in your journal to memorize. Speak it after you have written it in your journal. Do you have a simple melody to sing or your scripture words? Go on, give it a go! I remember one Christmas season several years ago, my sons and I picked Christmas carol melodies and sang scripture to them. As we were challenged to rap/sing the verse to align with the melody, we got the giggles.

Laughter is good medicine.

I have simple phrases and melodies I go to when I need a boost during the day.

'Give thanks to the Lord, for He is good. His love endures forever' is one I sing when needing a little smile.

For he enjoys his faithful lovers. He adorns the humble with his beauty
and he loves to give them the victory.
Psalm 149:4 TPT

What is God highlighting to you today? It could be a blessing that would encourage one another. Write it in your journal. Send it to someone. I would love to receive an encouraging word.

So grateful for this time each day! I chose the words 'beautiful' and 'compassionate'. I started practicing the 'body blessing' and now I do not curse myself with negative internal dialogue about all my attributes that fall short of the world's definition. Your prayers for me are so meaningful to me. Thank you so much! E., Alabama

Joy Key: Listen to God and listen to others – listen for the Jesus in others.

19. Community for Eternity

I am an introvert and I love people. Is this an oxymoron? When I was doing stand-up comedy for corporate events, I would soak in the tub until I visualized a great set or resembled a pale raisin. I am grateful for both immersion in community and immersion with God, alone. I believe Jesus modeled this for us. He modeled loving God and loving people, setting time apart to pray and be with God alone.

Time alone and time with others. Like trees. Trees appear to be standing by themselves, but their root systems tell a different story.

I live in Alabama. This state is covered with a wide variety of trees. Thick and in various stages of life, they outnumber the population 70 to 1, dominating most of the land on the mountain where I live.

I discovered a book in a quaint bookstore in Galway, Ireland, *The Hidden Life of Trees: What They Feel, How They Communicate—Discoveries from A Secret World*

The author, Peter Wohlleben, a forest expert, explores the way trees support each other. I now see trees in a new light.

Trees communicate through their root systems to send warnings of threats, and for their fellow trees to thrive, sharing nutrients and water. They help each other. Who knew we could learn about community from trees?

Think about it. Their life is usually spent in the same place and they often live much longer than us. Old trees and young trees help each other. Thy are not self-focused, but community-focused.

Think ecosystem; all things working together for life and purpose. God designed us to work together.

If we are open to it, we can learn a better approach to community life from trees. I will share more on this in the Rooted chapter.

You may already be surrounded by a forest of people. Pray and ask God for multiple generations of friends to fill your life. At least three generations. I pray to have an open heart to build healthy relationships with neighbors and with three generations. This wisdom for joy is as ancient as God, the father of Abraham, Isaac, and Jacob.

Joy Key: Trust God and pray for and build relationships with 3 generations of friends.

20. Rest and Repeat

This key is about using all the keys to keep going to improve 1% each day. What keys stand out to strengthen your joy, to reset, reboot, get up, dust off, and go after life with a smile again?

As I mentioned in the previous chapter, many times, a dark critical spirit was stealing joy from the process of doing the work I loved. When I learned to relax, trust God and not care what others were thinking, I found my sweet spot.

"Give your burdens to the Lord, and he will take care of you. He will not permit the godly to slip and fall."
Psalms 55:22 NLT

Older now, I play piano and lead worship. When I am playing piano, the passion to learn a song keeps me practicing, to learn and overcome mistakes. I still make them, especially when I am learning. I call it 'falling off the wagon'. But I keep going and the love of music and worship stays with me, unhindered by demonic shame of 'falling off the wagon' while playing piano. And in time, with grace, I joyfully hit the mark as I play.

Learning this joy-filled way to excellence has speed bumps, pot holes, and an occasional skunk. Sweet thing is, I am never alone on the trip. God will send a person or two to run with, to encourage, as we learn to love and trust God together as we step out to do new things.

Derek Prince stated, "If you are a believer in Jesus Christ, there is a call and a purpose for your life. A great call."

We don't get to great overnight.

God has been God a long time. He is a master at working with imperfect people. As we love and forgive ourselves and others, we reflect His mercy and grace.

It is in Him we find the excellence we are looking for in ourselves and others. He is in us. He desires for us to reflect His nature. In Him is sweet perfection.

Joy Key: Rest and repeat the joy keys to draw closer to God.

21. Rooted: Trees Overcome Together

Years ago, I toured Alaska with friends. We took a boat tour of the beautiful mountains surrounding Skagway. The guide showed us breathtaking waterfalls over the sheer rock, and the forests of trees on the mountains. At one point, the tour guide asked us, "Do you wonder how the trees can grow on sheer rock?"

I hadn't wondered, until she pointed it out. (Note to self: lead with a question to get a brain's attention.) When she shared how, it touched my spirit, God was speaking through this insight.

The trees are thick on sheer rock mountains around the waterways of Skagway. The trees interlock their roots together as they grow. By weaving their root systems together, they can climb up the mountain together. What would seem impossible for one, is made possible, together.

I have chill bumps as I write this. I witnessed a powerful life lesson as I looked at those trees. God's beautiful creation is demonstrating how to overcome mountains!

—·—

We can overcome together.

—·—

Alabama is an arborist's delight. We have so many types and numbers of trees. One estimate is a quarter of a billion trees in the state. There are 22 varieties of oaks in Alabama. I am declaring from Alabama for our nation to hunger for righteousness together!

—·—

We are designed to do life together. I have learned the beauty, power and vulnerability in this fact.

It is like God has this huge jigsaw puzzle and we are each a puzzle piece in God's great big multi-generational, multi-cultural, multi-dimensional puzzle. If you have ever completed a 500-piece puzzle, you know the sweet satisfaction of every piece in its place.

If I can envision that, I can celebrate the great worth of each piece.

Imagine many billion people all coming together to make a way for the returning of Yeshua/Jesus to earth. It is pretty awesome to be a piece of that picture.

God has given me a passion to see all of us in unity with Him. Imagine unity in families, to Ecclesia, to all of mankind loving and honoring God together.

My parents were deeply committed partners. Their marriage launched at the beginning of the space race and spanned over six decades, accompanied by mom's two favorite beverages - coffee and vodka. It was a roller coaster of historical events and emotions. This duo transitioned from their careers during the space race to running a successful multi-site antique business for over two decades. They married in Alabama, after four years, moved to Texas, after decades in Texas, they moved to Ohio for 18 months to help me and my sons during that rough divorce season. Finally moving from Ohio to Alabama for their last chapter. They grew deep roots with each other. Their desire for grand-bonding grew steadily as they grew older. Grand bonding between grandparents and grandchildren. (I had a very strong grand-bond with my dad's parents.)

Multi-generational friendships are a life enriching thing, perhaps one of the greatest.

Now, my father and my oldest son, his namesake, spend many hours together. More grand-bonding.

Dad, recently widowed, likes being independent. He told me many times how he loved mom and enjoyed taking care of her. Before my mom passed, she diminished in her mental and physical abilities dramatically. When she couldn't stand, dad couldn't lift her any more. Dad knew he couldn't do life alone. In this season, while he was hiring care for mom, ultimately it was his grandson who was there to catch him when he collapsed. (He had taken a fall earlier in the day on grass, without a scrape. But thin blood created a hemorrhage in a kidney, he was bleeding internally). Grandson Max called 911, then me. Through thick and thin the precious pair of Maxes continue to share time together. I loved caring for mom and sharing this time with Max and hospice. When my dad took a fall requiring hospitalization, we had two down. My sister drove from Texas and devoted weeks to serve through this time. We were able to help our parents together. With Max's other grandmother in her last days in hospice, he was able to go to Ohio to see her and his dad.

I don't fully grasp it all, but I trust God is working to touch hearts and work things for good in the timing of these events.

During this family shaking, a 21-Day, Isaiah 62 fast for Israel was taking place. It is the first time in known history that millions from around the world were all praying for Israel at the same time. The tensions continue in Israel as I write. Lord, I pray, please prepare us for these days ahead. I pray your perfect will and timing.

The Spirit and the bride say, "Come." Let anyone who hears this say, "Come." Let anyone who is thirsty come. Let anyone who desires drink freely from the water of life. God's word is true.

Rev. 22:17

Forgiving past wounds and repenting from wrong ways is a journey to joy. Forgiveness between our fellow man, and nations, could impact our life and history as never before. Pray for your nation and Israel. Your prayers matter.

We need God's love and wisdom to navigate this time.

Years ago, when I returned home after that Alaska tour, I found this quote from Dr. Martin Luther King, Jr. in my desk. It affirms what I saw with the trees on the mountains by Skagway in Alaska.

"All this is simply to say that all life is interrelated. We are caught in an inescapable network of mutuality; tied in a single garment of destiny. Whatever affects one directly, affects all indirectly. As long as there is poverty in this world, no man can be totally rich even if he has a billion dollars. As long as diseases are rampant and millions of people cannot expect to live more than twenty or thirty years, no man can be totally healthy, even if he just got a clean bill of health from the finest clinic in America. Strangely enough, I can never be what I ought to be until you are what you ought to be. You can never be what you ought to be until I am what I ought to be."

Martin Luther King, Jr.

I recently shared the Resilience message in Ohio. It took me back to the first time. My first motivational talk outside my workplace was in Nashville. Not knowing what to name this topic, I shared the content outline with my friend, Dr. Belinda Gore. When she heard it, she gave me the name: Resilience.

 Another friend, Heidi, had heard I was going to speak in Nashville. While we were walking in her neighborhood, she asked what I was speaking on. I answered her with the enthusiasm of a proud mama sharing the name of her first born, "Resilience." I stated with a big smile.

 "Brazil Nuts?" she asked.

I repeated Resilience. She responded, "I think Brazil Nuts would be more interesting."

Heidi's observation now opens my Resilience message each time I share it. After saying 'Brazil Nuts' repeatedly at corporate events across the country, I got curious about them.   I did a little research and discovered God had hidden something for us.

The Brazil Nut tree is one of the tallest and longest-living trees in the rainforest. The Brazil Nut tree could be the mascot for Resilience. Also, Brazil Nuts are rich in selenium. Healthline.com lists selenium benefits including: battling free radicals from oxidative stress, and disorders including **memory issues**[1]. This means eating Brazil Nuts (in moderation) can help your mind overcome toxic thinking. God you're amazing.

You may have noticed a few 22's scattered throughout this book. Sweet home Alabama is the 22nd state in the union. There are 22 varieties of oaks in Alabama.   This book gives you 22 keys to joy. There is a light post that wears a 22 label outside my dad's place. This number has been highlighted to me for years, followed me to Alabama, and has been in front of me as I prepared this book.

I will place on his shoulder the key to the house of David; what he opens no one can shut, and what he shuts no one can open.

Isaiah: 22:22, NIV

When applying joy keys to your life, you can unlock your inheritance as a child of God. As a child of God, you inherited a joy perspective. Like a child receiving balloons and seeking solid rock truths to stand on, you are called 'up' in God's presence in peace and joy.

As you are celebrating God, God is celebrating you.

We can get distracted, but He delights in seeing our faith, hope and joy grow lingering in His love. You are designed to overcome in authority as a child of God.

1.https://www.healthline.com/nutrition/selenium-benefits#2.-May-reduce-your-risk-of-certain-cancers

Keep going. You have God and God has got it all...including abundant joy!

As the Father loved Me, I also have loved you; abide in My love. 10 If you keep My commandments, you will abide in My love, just as I have kept My Father's commandments and abide in His love.
"These things I have spoken to you, that My joy may remain in you, and that your joy may be full. This is My commandment, that you love one another as I have loved you."

John 15:9-12 NKJV

Joy Key: Look and discover God in every part of your life.

Emmanuel. God is with us.

22. Gold Mine

The enemy will want to distract you and kill your joy.

You are designed for joy to overcome.

To live this out takes deliberate choices every day. It is a discipline, even a battle. There is gold in the process.

Don't give up. In Napoleon Hill's classic *Think and Grow Rich*, written during the Great Depression, he tells this story of a gold miner. Let's look at the story:

"One of the most common causes of failure is the habit of quitting when one is overtaken by temporary defeat. Every person is guilty of this mistake at one time or another.

An uncle of R.U. Darby was caught by the "gold fever" in the gold-rush days, and went west to "dig and grow rich." He had heard that more gold has been mined from the brains of men than has ever been taken from the earth. He staked a claim and went to work with pick and shovel.

After weeks of labor, he was rewarded by the discovery of the shining ore. He needed machinery to bring the ore to the surface. Quietly, he covered up the mine, retraced his footsteps to his home in Williamsburg, Maryland, told his relatives and a few neighbors of the "strike." They got together money for the needed machinery, had it shipped. The uncle and Darby went back to work the mine.

The first car of ore was mined, and shipped to a smelter. The returns proved they had one of the richest mines in Colorado! A few more cars of that ore would clear the debts. Then would come the big killing in profits.

Down went the drills! Up went the hopes of Darby and Uncle! Then something happened! The vein of gold ore disappeared! They had come to the end of the rainbow, and the pot of gold was no longer there! They drilled on, desperately trying to pick up the vein again — all to no avail.

Finally, they decided to quit. They sold the machinery to a junk man for a few hundred dollars, and took the train back home. The junk man called in a mining engineer to look at the mine and do a little calculating. The engineer advised that the project had failed because the owners were not familiar with "fault lines." His calculations showed that the vein would be found just three feet from where the Darbys had stopped drilling. That is exactly where it was found!

The junk man took millions of dollars in ore from the mine, because he knew enough to seek expert counsel before giving up."

In 1 Kings 3:3-15, young King Solomon was sleeping when God asked what he desired. Solomon loved God and wanted to honor God and to lead wisely. This answer pleased God and He gave him wisdom but also wealth and much more. The Word says Solomon 'loved the Lord'.

When we love God, we can trust His wisdom. He is a loving father, a patient teacher, a precious husband of great provision, love, justice, hope, wisdom, and shalom. Our faith + God can shift the mountains of confusion and darkness to align with God's power to see all ways to glorify Him. Glory is in Him and Him alone.

Pride will block intimacy with God. Fear of what others will think interferes with intimacy with God.

The Bait of Satan by John Bevere is a great resource to identify and purge the wickedness of pride. Pride is the root of offense (Prov. 13:10), it puts walls up that don't belong, keeping healthy relationships from forming. It creates unhealthy narcissistic like thinking. Both selfish and self-hatred come from prideful, self-centered thinking.

Humility and faith please God.

Practicing the keys in this book, God will show you His perspective and a strategy to extract pride. Pride is sneaky. Be persistent in seeking His word and His way.

⁓❦ —·— ❦⁓

Know your armor as a child of God and wear it 24/7.

⁓❦ —·— ❦⁓

When you step out to draw close to God, you will be tested. Expect enemy attack on your thoughts, preying on self-doubt and rallying you to doubt God. This battle isn't just in your mind. Well-meaning friends and relatives can be used by satan. Past emotional wounds can be open doors to distort your view of others and yourself. Use your keys to conquer the false beliefs and spiritual attacks with love, in spirit and truth, to see your way to Yeshua/Jesus.

I am inviting you to fully trust God for the greatest possible outcome in all circumstances. The wise counselor of Holy Spirit is with you as long as you live.

Joy Key: The fear of the Lord is the beginning of Wisdom. Seek God in all things.

The Road is the Joy

'I can do all things through Christ who strengthens me.'

Phil. 4:13

Growing closer to God is a joy practice. With faith in God the hard things will become easier, the worry will diminish, the fear will be short lived, and the awareness of God's powerful love will grow you into maturity and authority.

Nehemiah said, Go and enjoy choice food and sweet drinks, and send some to those who have nothing prepared. This day is holy to our Lord. Do not grieve, for **the joy of the Lord is your strength.**
Neh. 8:10 NIV

In this text, Ezra was speaking to the men, women and people who could understand God's word. When Ezra opened the sacred word of God, the people stood and remained standing, listening to the Word of God. They were weeping, worshiping and agreeing as they learned and understood the Word.

I believe this is how God wants us. Hungry to learn His word and love Him more deeply.

Life with God is an adventure and an exercise in getting comfortable with being uncomfortable. The process of growing with God means knowing His deep joy and freedom. Knowing God, we live a life of gratitude and expanded horizons. It is living a life of the impossible becoming possible. It is living a life of forgiving yourself and others. It is living a life of letting go of disappointments in exchange for God's better plan. It is living a life of healing as you go, often imperfectly, growing and knowing God is with you every step of the way.

Those who look to Him for help will be radiant with joy; no shadow of shame will darken their faces. Ps 34:5 NLT

Your faith pleases God.

Thank you for making room in your life for this book.

Rejoice in the Lord always. I will say it again: Rejoice! Let your gentleness be evident to all. The Lord is near. Do not be anxious about anything, but in every situation, by prayer and petition, with thanksgiving, present your requests to God. And the peace of God, which transcends all understanding, will guard your hearts and your minds in Christ Jesus.

Phil. 4:4-7 NIV

May you know Him well and experience His greatest joy.

Epilogue

August 29, 2023

Just Love. Two powerful words. I am still stunned by the news we received yesterday. Back Story. In July 2022, our family of four, (Max, George, their dad Jeff, and me), gathered to support our friend David & his family at his brother's funeral. We later regathered with their family and friends at a musical tribute & celebration of life.

When I was packing for this trip, Holy Spirit urged me to take extra cash. Not understanding why, I obeyed. I stayed with a friend in Ohio whose band was playing at a steak dinner (cash only) benefit for veterans on Jeff's birthday. I realized what the extra cash was for and invited Jeff and his mom, and the boys over to celebrate Jeff. The band sang a joyful Happy Birthday over him. Jeff and I had reconnected as friends. The power of forgiveness is priceless- years in coming, but so worth it for our family. This visit to Ohio saw time together as a family, in grieving, comforting, and then celebrating Jeff turning 68.

Jeff's 69th birthday was on July 29, 2023. We celebrated him virtually. My sons called and sang a Happy Birthday duet. I sent Birthday blessings and received his wish for a spice cake, along with his humor, a need for the fire department to put out the inferno of candles.

Yesterday, after receiving the news, Max and I sat on the couch together in shock. I called my dear friend Linda to pray. We did and she added her wise counsel, drink a sweetened cup of tea, it will help.

The news we received still hurts my heart as I write - Jeff had died. A police officer asked for Max's information to give to the coroner. The loss of my mom and Jeff's mom in June is still fresh. We didn't see this one coming.

Jeff loved the Beatles. The last text I sent him was a link to Dolly Parton's new release "Let it Be".

Grieving has a promise in its time. Joy. (Is. 61:3)

I trust Him as I grieve. I know He is with me, and I am aching for my sons as they navigate this loss. I have full faith we will make it through this hard thing. I see He has us in the palm of His hand.

When you get hard news, God's word, prayer with faithful friends and family (and a sweet cup of tea) comforts the soul.

I don't have any fancy words to add. I am literally going back to these keys to walk this out one day at a time. I am in the Word, I am speaking it out loud and I am finding simple joys and giving thanks every day. Breathing healing breath while I am comforted by Holy Spirit. This is my faith walk with God. Our family will get through this growing closer to each other and to God. I can't imagine it any other way.

Photos

with my sons in Huntsville Al.

Pepper

Jo Ann, with her husband Nathan, son Aydin,
me and George, with his long selfie arm

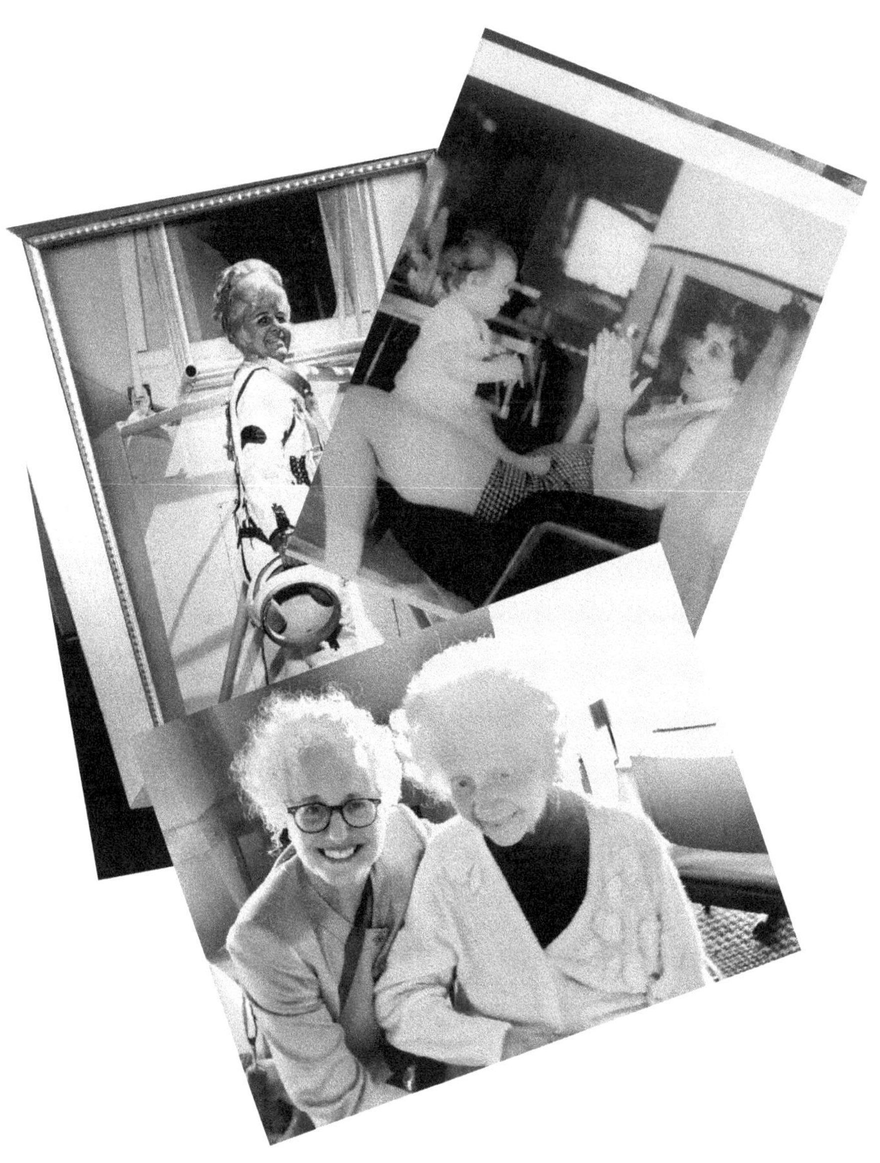

Mom and me at the beginning, then on Mother's Day 2023, and during her 'high profile days'.

Jo Ann loved board games.

Our family with BB, my amazing grandmother.

Dawn Holley

P.O. Box 753
Huntsville Al 35804

dawnofresilience.com